David Richardson is a illustrator, graphic designer and and bred in West Yorkshire, before going to art college in Staffordshire. He moved to London after leaving university and began his reportorial illustration journey around the capital. A successful career in the magazine industry saw him rise to the role of Group Creative Director of several award-winning TV titles in print and online.

Colin Tough is a journalist, editor and Internet pioneer. He began his career in Scottish newspapers, editing his first title at the age of 19, before moving to London and the magazine industry. Having edited a range of print titles, he helped launch many of the UK's first websites before returning to ink-on-paper magazines as editor-in-chief of the UK's best-selling TV titles, What's On TV, TV Times and TV & Satellite Week.

Copyright © 2023 David Richardson and Colin Tough

The moral right of the authors has been asserted.

All rights reserved. No part of this publication may be reproduced, stored in a retrieval system, or transmitted, in any form or by any means, without the prior permission in writing of the authors or publisher.

A Wymbridge Publishing paperback
Email: wymbridge@gmail.com

ISBN: 9798868011634

*For Alex, James, Katie,
Chris and Alexander*

The Walking Guide to
LONDON FILM SITES

Illustrations and Book Design by David Richardson
Written by Colin Tough

Enjoy the walks Annie!
David Richardson

introduction

The bustling heart of London, where history and tradition blend seamlessly with modernity, has been a favourite canvas for creative film producers for more than a century.

From the cobbled streets of Victorian-era dramas to the gleaming skyscrapers of contemporary thrillers, London's diverse landscapes have played starring roles in hundreds of films.

The Walking Guide to London Film Sites invites you on a captivating journey through this cinematic wonderland, one step at a time, taking you on a tour of London's most iconic and lesser-known film locations.

From the enchanting magical world of Diagon Alley where Harry Potter prepared for life at Hogwarts, and the bustling streets of Notting Hill where Hugh Grant and Julia Roberts found love, to the iconic London landmarks that witnessed superheroes and villains do battle, we'll trace the footsteps of your favourite characters.

Plus, the walks also allow you to experience the real London as they offer a unique lens on the vibrant neighbourhoods, charming parks and hidden gems where the films were shot and that make London one of the world's greatest cities.

So your journey is as enjoyable as possible, it's worth remembering a few things:

▶ Journey lengths will vary depending on the speed you walk – the timings we offer are simply a guide. They also don't include the length of time you may choose to spend at each location or the time you may have to wait for a Tube train or boat.

▶ The map illustrations are not to scale and are simply to aid direction.

▶ Film information may include some spoilers. If you haven't seen a film, and plan to watch it in the future, you might want to skip the plot explanation.

So, pull on your walking shoes and grab your book to begin your cinematic journey through the heart of London and discover where the magic of the silver screen comes alive on the city's streets.

Colin Tough

contents

SOUTH OF THE RIVER

Skyfall
Albert Embankment.. p3

28 Days Later
Westminster Bridge... p5

Fantastic Four - Rise of the Silver Surfer
The London Eye... p7

The Bourne Ultimatum
Waterloo Station.. p9

DETOUR The Pirates of the Carribean: On Stranger Tides
Hampton Court Palace.. p11

Legend
Roupell Street.. p13

Love Actually
Gabriel's Wharf... p15

Harry Potter and the Half Blood Prince
The Millennium Bridge... p17

Lock Stock and Two Smoking Barrels
Park Street... p19

Bridget Jones' Diary
The Globe Tavern... p20

Spider-Man: Far From Home
Tower Bridge.. p21

Thor: The Dark World
The Royal Naval College.. p23

Bridgerton
Ranger's House.. p25

DETOUR The World is Not Enough
The O2 Arena... p27

WEST CENTRAL

Rocketman
Regency Cafe... p31

Die Another Day
Buckingham Palace.. p33

Downton Abbey
Bridgewater House... p35

Darkest Hour
Churchill War Rooms... p37

The Thirty Nine Steps
Big Ben Tower.. p38

Octopussy
Old War Office Building... p39

V for Vendetta
Trafalgar Square... p41

Skyfall
The National Gallery.. p42

Batman Begins
Garrick Theatre... p43

DETOUR SCENES IN THE SQUARE
Leicester Square... p45

Kingsman: The Secret Service
Savile Row.. p45

84 Charing Cross Road
Charing Cross Road.. p47

An American Werewolf in London
Tottenham Court Road Tube Station p49

My Fair Lady
Covent Garden p51

The Fifth Element
The Royal Opera House p53

The Long Good Friday
The Savoy Hotel p55

GoldenEye
Somerset House p57

Harry Potter and the Philosopher's (Sorcerer's) Stone
Australia House p59

EAST CENTRAL

The Da Vinci Code
Temple Church p63

Snatch
Ye Olde Mitre p65

Four Weddings and a Funeral
St Bartholomew the Great p66

Mary Poppins
St. Paul's Cathedral p67

Mary Poppins Returns
The Royal Exchange p69

Harry Potter and the Philosopher's (Sorcerer's) Stone
Leadenhall Market p71

Guardians of the Galaxy
The Lloyd's Building p73

NORTH CENTRAL

Notting Hill
Westbourne Park Road p77

Notting Hill
Portobello Road p79

Love Actually
St Lukes Mews p81

DETOUR The Gentleman
The Princess Victoria p83

Paddington Bear
Paddington Station p85

Sherlock
North Gower Street p87

Harry Potter and the Philosopher's (Sorcerer's) Stone
London Zoo Reptile House p89

DETOUR Fantastic Beasts: The Crimes of Grindelwald
Highgate Cemetery p91

Paddington Bear
Chalot Crescent p93

Harry Potter and the Philosopher's (Sorcerer's) Stone
King's Cross Station p95

Harry Potter and the Philosopher's (Sorcerer's) Stone
St Pancras Renaissance Hotel p97

Harry Potter and the Order of the Phoenix
Claremont Square p99

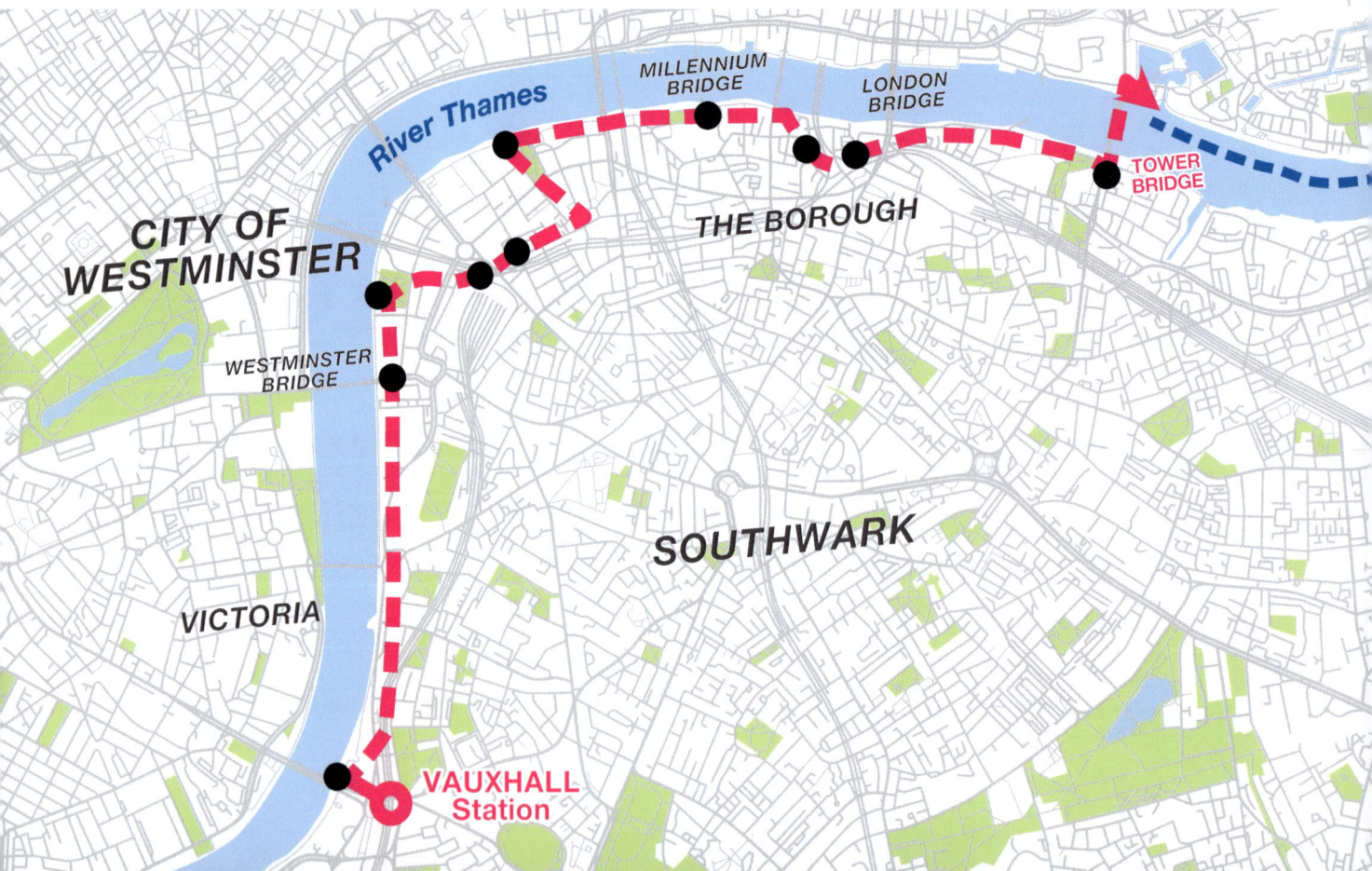

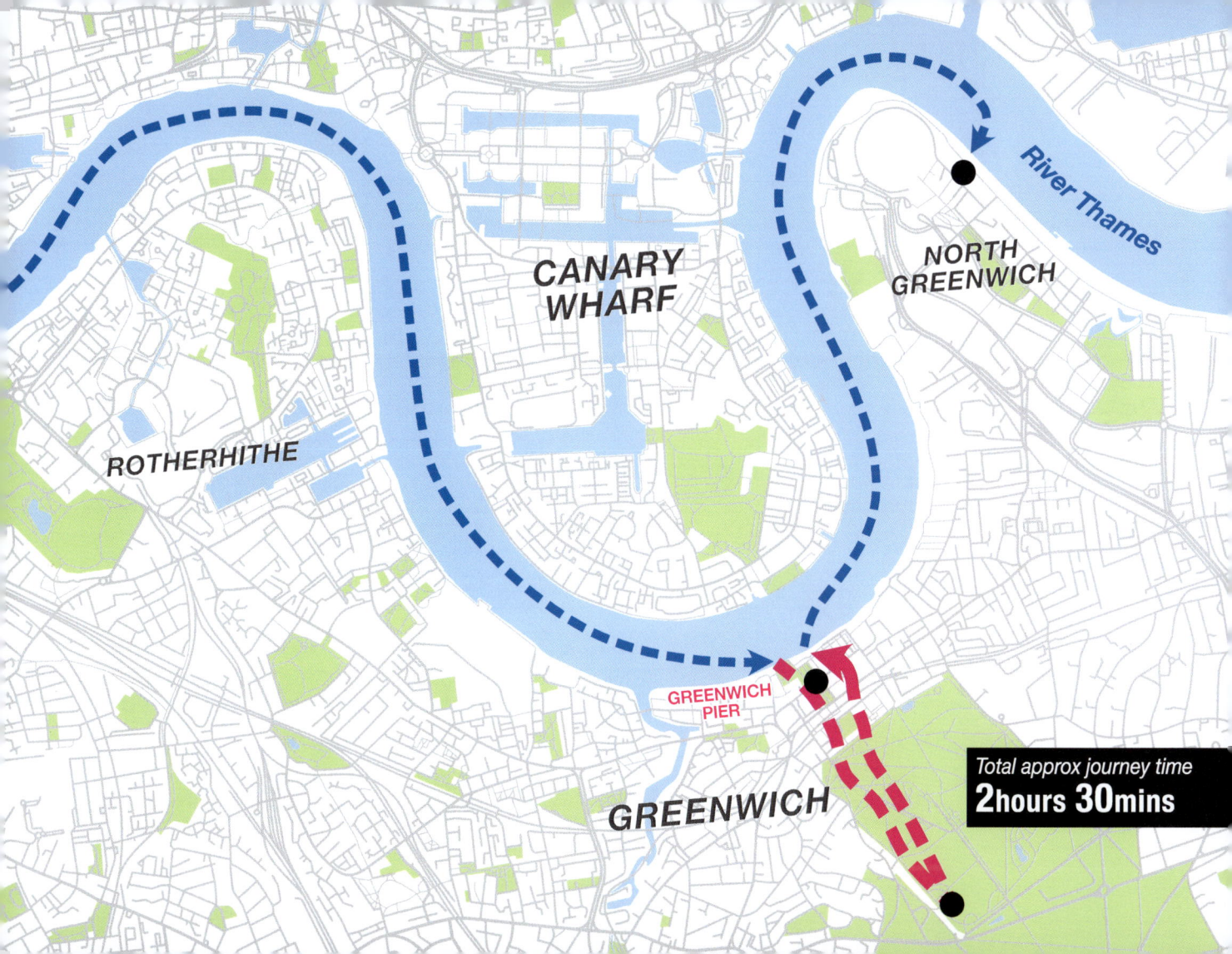

▶▶ THE WALKING GUIDE TO LONDON FILM SITES

SOUTH OF THE RIVER

Take a cinematic journey along the south bank of the Thames, where celebrated scenes from films including Skyfall, Bridget Jones's Diary and Spider-Man: Far From Home come to life

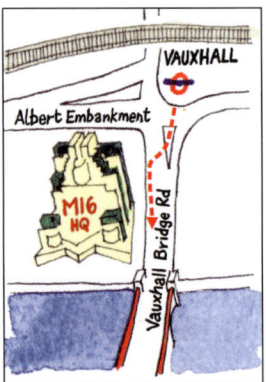

SKYFALL (2012)
MI6 HQ, 85 Albert Embankment SE1 7TY

Getting there
Start your journey by taking the train to Vauxhall Tube Station, leaving by the Albert Embankment exit. Turn right and head across **Vauxhall Bridge Road/ Kennington Lane**. The MI6 building is in front of you. You can walk over Vauxhall Bridge to get another view of the building. *(journey time 2 mins)*

The plot
In *Skyfall*, the MI6 HQ at Vauxhall is attacked and destroyed by a terrorist group. The attack is carried out by cyber-terrorist Raoul Silva who hacks into the MI6 computer system. The illusion of an explosion was created using a mix of practical and visual effects.

Other starring roles
The building was first seen in a Bond film, *GoldenEye* (1995), the year after its official opening by Queen Elizabeth II in July 1994.

In *The World Is Not Enough* (1999) a bomb is detonated in the building killing British oil tycoon Sir Robert King, a friend of 007's boss M, and damaging a portion of the structure.

Background
The MI6 building, officially known as the SIS Building, serves as the headquarters of British intelligence. MI6's main focus is gathering intelligence about foreign governments, organisations and individuals that pose a threat to UK national security. It also works to disrupt and prevent terrorist attacks and other forms of criminal activity that could harm the UK and its citizens. It has officers operating around the world and works closely with other UK intelligence agencies such as MI5 and GCHQ. The building, constructed between 1989 and 1994, has 10 floors above ground and three below. The exterior of the building features a distinctive design, with a curved, glass-covered facade. The building took the place of Century House at 100 Westminster Bridge Road which was the service's headquarters for 30 years until 1994. While its role was technically an official secret, its location was known to every London tour guide, bus and taxi driver, along with the KGB.

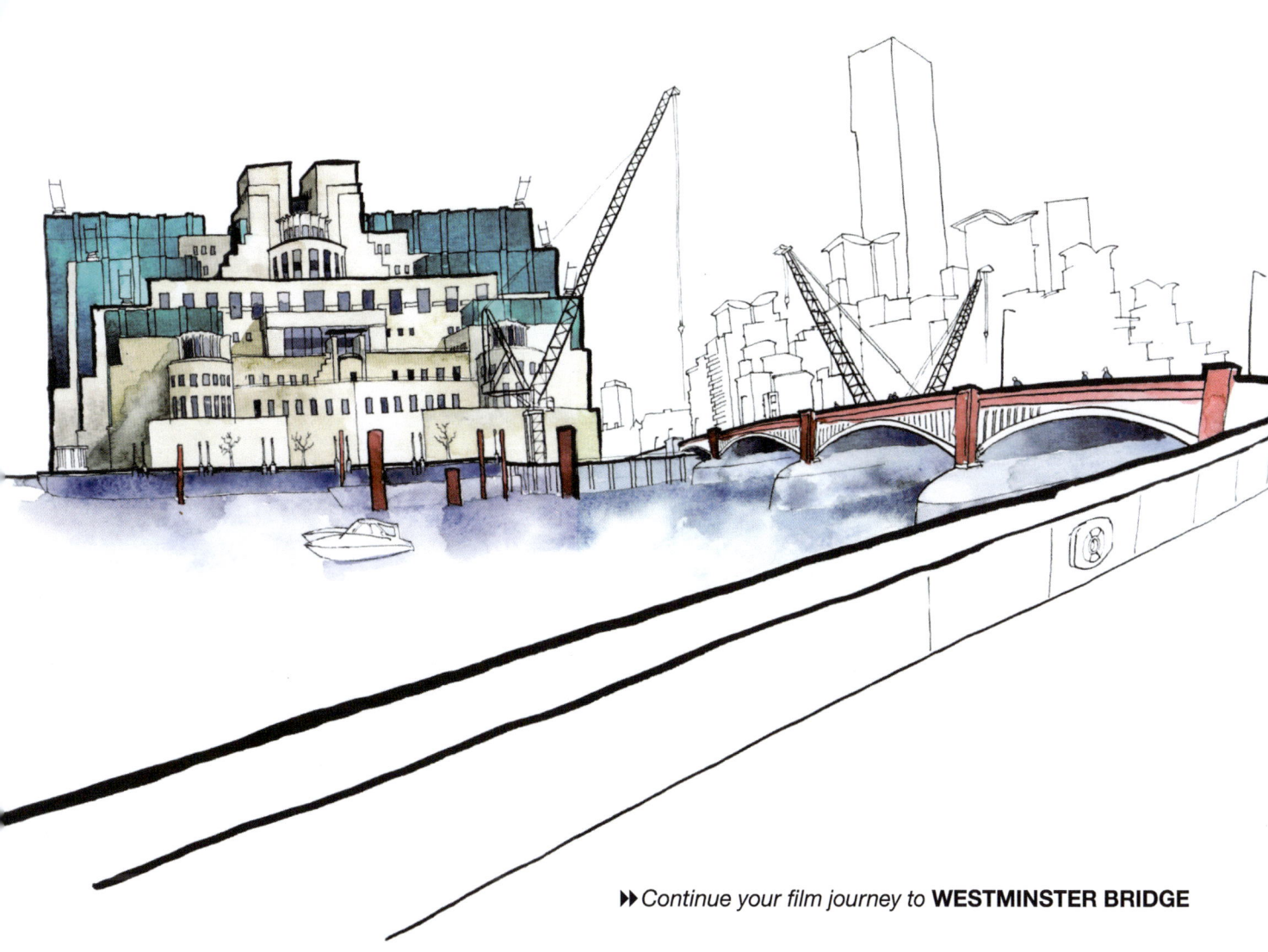
▶▶ Continue your film journey to **WESTMINSTER BRIDGE**

▶▶ THE WALKING GUIDE TO LONDON FILM SITES

28 DAYS LATER (2002)
Westminster Bridge SW1A 2JH

Getting there
From the MI6 building on the south of the river, continue along the **Albert Embankment** as it becomes **Lambeth Palace Road**. Passing Lambeth Bridge on the left, keep to the pedestrian path along the river at the back of St Thomas' Hospital. Westminster Bridge is up the steps just after St Thomas'. *(journey time 18 mins)*

The plot
28 Days Later tells the story of the aftermath of a highly contagious deadly virus, called "Rage", that has been unleashed on Britain. The film's hero Jim (Cillian Murphy) wakes from a coma in a deserted St Thomas' Hospital. He wanders out into the city, which is eerie and silent, showing signs of a catastrophe having taken place. As he crosses Westminster Bridge, the scene sets the bleak tone for the rest of the film. Central London was not shut down for filming. Instead, the location team got up very early in the morning and began shooting soon after dawn before the city became busy.

Other starring roles
In the James Bond film *Die Another Day* (2002), 007 receives a key from M that opens the door to a secret part of MI6, an abandoned Tube station. The door is located at the south end of Westminster Bridge.

The bridge is the location for the finale of another Bond film, *Spectre* (2015), as 007 shoots down Blofeld's helicopter, which crashes onto the bridge.

Background
For more than 600 years, from the 12th century until the 18th century, the nearest Thames bridge to London Bridge was many miles away in Kingston. Any proposals to build a new bridge downstream from Kingston were forcefully opposed by London Bridge's owners, the City of London, and the Company of Watermen, which had a monopoly of the river's ferrymen. A bridge was finally built at Putney in 1729 and the construction of Westminster Bridge was approved a decade later, finally opening in 1750. By the middle of the 19th century, however, the original bridge was suffering structural problems and a decision was made to rebuild it. The new bridge, designed by Thomas Page, was constructed between 1835 and 1862. It's painted verdant green as a homage to the seats in the nearby House of Commons. In 2017 a terrorist attack took place on the bridge, which resulted in five deaths.

▶▶ *Continue your film journey to* **THE LONDON EYE**

▶▶ THE WALKING GUIDE TO LONDON FILM SITES

FANTASTIC FOUR: RISE OF THE SILVER SURFER (2007)
The London Eye SE1 7PB

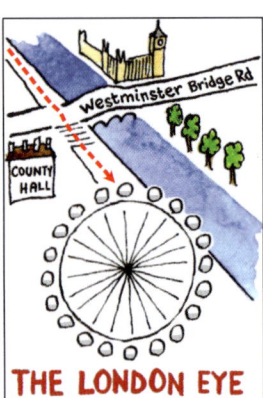

Getting there
Cross to the west side of Westminster Bridge, descend the stairs down the side of County Hall, and walk along the Embankment to the Eye.
(journey time 4 mins)

The plot
The Fantastic Four must again save the world in *Rise of the Silver Surfer* as the intergalactic herald the Silver Surfer comes to Earth to prepare it for destruction by the evil Galactus. At the London Eye, the Silver Surfer creates a crater in preparation for Galactus's arrival. The Fantastic Four appear and during the battle the team must prevent the London Eye toppling into the Thames.

Other starring roles
Since its construction, the London Eye has become a firm favourite with film companies who have used it as a location that instantly anchors a movie in the British capital. *28 Days Later* (2002), *Thunderbirds* (2004) and *Harry Potter and the Order of the Phoenix* (2007) are just a few examples where the iconic landmark has appeared in the background.

Set in medieval London, *A Knight's Tale* (2001) even pays homage to the Eye by featuring a wooden version of the structure in an establishing shot of 14th century London.

Background
The London Eye is a giant Ferris wheel on the South Bank of the River Thames in London, consisting of 32 sealed air-conditioned capsules. When it was built it was the world's tallest wheel and also London's highest public viewing point. Several other wheels now surpass its height, however, and the 804ft (245m) high observation deck on the 72nd floor of The Shard snatched the second record away from it in 2013. It continues to be one of the most popular paid tourist attractions in the United Kingdom, however, with more than 3.5 million visitors annually. Construction began on the London Eye, originally named the Millennium Wheel as it was built to celebrate the new millennium, in 1998, and the wheel was opened to the public by the Prime Minister, Tony Blair, on 31 December 1999. The London Eye was originally intended to be a temporary attraction, with a five-year lease. However, it proved so popular that it was granted permanent status by the local council in 2002.

▶▶ *Continue your film journey to* **WATERLOO STATION**

▶▶ THE WALKING GUIDE TO LONDON FILM SITES

THE BOURNE ULTIMATUM (2007)
Waterloo Station SE1 8SW

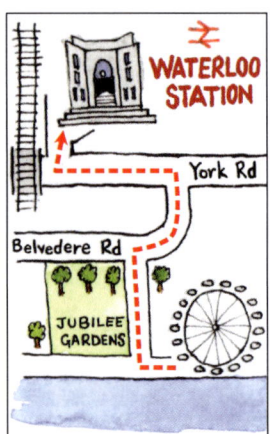

Getting there
From the London Eye, walk up the path opposite the wheel, with Jubilee Gardens on your left. Cross **Belvedere Road** and continue up to the main thoroughfare, **York Road**. Cross the road and turn left towards the railway bridge at the bottom of the road. Turn right just before the bridge and you'll see the entrance to the station.
(journey time 9 mins)

The plot
In **The Bourne Ultimatum** Waterloo Station is where Simon Ross (Paddy Considine), a journalist who is investigating Jason Bourne's past, is assassinated. Bourne (Matt Damon) attempts to protect the journalist from unseen gunmen as crowds bustle around them in the packed station. Eventually, however, Ross is killed by a black ops assassin named Paz (Édgar Ramírez), who works for the CIA.

Other starring roles
In **Living** (2022), Williams (Oscar-nominated Bill Nighy) makes the daily journey through Waterloo Station and across Waterloo Bridge to his job at the Greater London County Council. In reality, however, the council's offices at County Hall were on the same side of the bridge as Waterloo Station.

The station has also been used as the location for a number of other films, including **Sliding Doors** (1998), **Absolutely Fabulous: The Movie** (2016) and **Man Up** (2015).

Background
Waterloo Station, designed by William Tite, is the busiest railway station in the UK. When it opened in 1848, however, there were just 14 trains to and from the station each day.

From 1854, the station was the terminus for the London Necropolis Railway, which carried corpses and mourners to the newly opened Brookwood Cemetery, at the time the largest in the world. Waterloo was a major terminal station for troops during World War One and Two and the impressive main pedestrian entrance, the Victory Arch (known as Exit 5), is a memorial to those killed in the conflicts. World War Two also saw Waterloo Station suffer significant damage due to bombings and after the war the station was restored and modernised. The station was the first London terminus for Eurostar trains, from 1994 until 2007, when they transferred to St Pancras.

9

▸▸ *Continue your film journey to* **ROUPELL STREET**
Or take a detour to **HAMPTON COURT PALACE**

SUGGESTED DETOUR

Pirates of the Caribbean: On Stranger Tides (2011)
Hampton Court Palace, 1709 Hampton Ct Rd, Molesey, East Molesey KT8 9AU

Getting there
While visiting Waterloo Station, you can make a detour to Hampton Court Palace. Take the South Western Railway train from the station to Hampton Court. Turn right onto the bridge and the palace is on the other side. *(journey time 30-37 mins one way)*

The plot
Hampton Court Palace was used as a filming location for the fourth instalment of the *Pirates of the Caribbean* film series, with the palace representing St James's Palace, where Captain Jack Sparrow is arrested and brought before King George II.

Other starring roles
The Netflix spin-off *Queen Charlotte: A Bridgerton Story* (2023) used locations in and around Hampton Court, including the Privy Garden, Clock Court, Base Court and the Orangery.

Many scenes in the multi-award winning film *The Favourite* (2018), about two cousins who vie to be court favourite of Queen Anne (Olivia Coleman) in 18th century England, were shot in the palace, where Anne herself once lived.

Background
The transformation of what had been an ordinary country house into a sumptuous palace was begun by Cardinal Thomas Wolsey, King Henry VIII's chief minister, in 1514, but when Wolsey fell out of favour he offered the building to the king in an attempt to ingratiate himself. It became a favourite of Henry and he brought all six of his wives to the palace by the Thames. Jane Seymour sadly died at the palace after giving birth to the king's son, Edward (later Edward VI), and Catherine Howard was arrested there before being found guilty of adultery and treason and executed at the Tower of London.

After his defeat in the Civil War, in 1647 Charles I was held under house arrest at Hampton Court. He escaped through the Privy Garden but was later recaptured and executed. The palace fell out of favour as a royal residence in the mid-18th century under George II and became a home for grace and favour residents before Queen Victoria decreed that it should be open to visitors in 1838. Tours are available daily.

▶▶ THE WALKING GUIDE TO LONDON FILM SITES

LEGEND (2015)
Roupell Street SE1 8TB

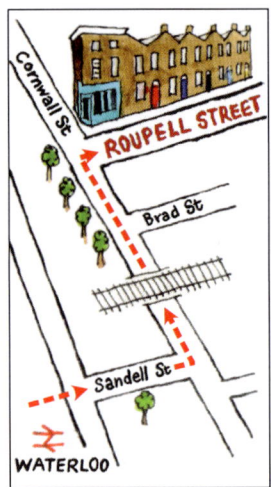

Getting there
Walk through Waterloo Station and descend the escalator opposite platforms 1-6. Leave the station and cross at the traffic lights to the other side of **Waterloo Road**. Turn down **Sandell Street**, the road just a few yards up on your left, and turn left under the bridge at the end of the street. Pass **Brad Street** on your right and **Roupell Street** is next on your right.
(journey time 5 mins)

The plot
Legend tells the true story of the Kray twins, the infamous London gangster brothers, both played by Tom Hardy. It follows their rise to prominence in the London underworld, their close relationship and their ultimate imprisonment. Roupell Street and the surrounding area played a major role in the film, as they offered a backdrop that has hardly changed since the 1960s, when the film is set. Whittlesey Street portrayed the Krays' real-life home in Bethnal Green. Theed Street also plays a major part in the drama.

Other starring roles
Roupell Street and the surrounding roads are a popular area for production companies filming period dramas, as it appears almost unchanged since the 19th century when Charles Dickens walked the streets. TV dramas such as **Mr Selfridge** (2013) and **Call the Midwife** (2012) have used the area, as have films such as **Mrs Harris Goes to Paris** (2022), starring Lesley Manville, and **See How They Run** (2022), with Sam Rockwell.

While **No Time to Die** (2021) sees James Bond (Daniel Craig) and Moneypenny (Naomie Harris) visit Q (Ben Wishaw) at his home in present-day Roupell Street.

Background
Roupell Street was built in the early 19th century as part of a development project by John Palmer Roupell, a wealthy landowner and developer. The street was designed to provide housing for working-class artisan families. Originally the surrounding streets were named after members of his family, but John Street, Richard Street and Catherine Street were changed to Theed Street, Whittlesey Street West and Whittlesey Street East, reportedly due to problems the names caused for postmen. Today, Roupell Street is a protected conservation area and its well-preserved architecture provides a glimpse into London's past.

▶▶ *Continue your film journey to* **GABRIEL'S WHARF**

▸▸ THE WALKING GUIDE TO LONDON FILM SITES

LOVE ACTUALLY (2003)
Gabriel's Wharf, Upper Ground SE1 9PP

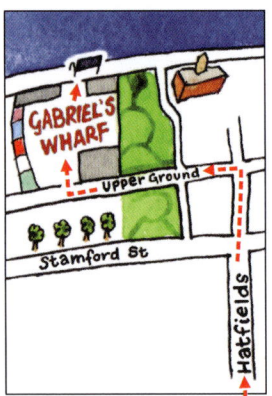

Getting there
Carry on walking away from Waterloo Station until you reach the far end of **Roupell Street**, passing The Kings Arms on your right. Turn left down **Hatfields** at the end and carry on across **Stamford Street**, down to **Upper Ground**. Here turn left, across **Broadwall** on your left and then past gardens on your left and right. Gabriel's Wharf is on your right. Walk through to reach the Thames Embankment.
(journey time 10 mins)

The plot
One of the many threads running through the film is the story of Daniel (Liam Neeson), who, following the recent death of his wife, Joanna, is trying to care for his stepson Sam (Thomas Brodie-Sangster). A key scene between the two takes place on a bench overlooking the Thames at Gabriel's Wharf, where the pair bond as they have a heart-to-heart about love.

Other starring roles
This stretch of the Thames is instantly recognisable from numerous TV shows and films, not least because it offers an unrivalled view of St Paul's Cathedral in the background.
In **Thor: The Dark World** (2013), the glass-walled restaurant with a stunning view of the London skyline where Thor's love interest astrophysicist Jane (Natalie Portman) has a date with Richard (Chris O'Dowd) is in the Oxo Tower, which overlooks Gabriel's Wharf.
The romantic drama **Last**

Chance Harvey (2008), starring Dustin Hoffman and Emma Thompson, features the stretch of the Thames Embankment from outside the National Theatre to Gabriel's Wharf.

Background

Gabriel's Wharf is an eclectic mix of shops, restaurants and galleries. The Oxo Tower next door was originally built as a power station for the Royal Mail in the late 19th century. In the 1920s, it was bought by the company who produced Oxo beef stock cubes, the Liebig Extract of Meat Company, who applied for permission to advertise their product with an illuminated sign. When the application was rejected, the company erected four sets of three vertically aligned windows, two circular and one in the shape of a cross which when light was shined from the windows spelled out the name of the company's beef cubes. The name of Barge House Street, behind the Oxo Tower, commemorates the old barge house and stairs where the Royal barge was housed from the days of Henry VII to Charles I.

▶▶ *Continue your film journey to* **THE MILLENNIUM BRIDGE**

▶▶ THE WALKING GUIDE TO LONDON FILM SITES

HARRY POTTER AND THE HALF-BLOOD PRINCE (2009)
The Millennium Bridge SE1 9JE

Getting there
Looking at the Thames from outside Gabriel's Wharf, turn right away from Waterloo, continue along the Embankment and walk under Blackfriars Bridge. Pass the chimney of the Tate Modern on your right and the Millennium Bridge is directly in front.
(journey time 10 mins)

The plot
The Millennium Bridge appears in the film as the location of a terrorist attack by Death Eaters. The attack was ordered by Lord Voldemort who had threatened to cause a mass Muggle killing if Cornelius Fudge didn't step down from his role as Minister for Magic. The Death Eaters circle the bridge, twisting and buckling the walkway until its cables snap. The bridge also appears in *Harry Potter and the Order of the Phoenix* (2007) when Harry flies over London with the Order on the way to Grimauld Place.

Other starring roles
With St Paul's Cathedral as a backdrop at one end of the bridge and the impressive Tate Modern at the other, the bridge provides a atmospheric location for films.

The Millennium Bridge stands in for the futuristic landscape of the planet Xandar in *Guardians of the Galaxy* (2014) as the wife of Rhomann Dey (John C Reilly) runs across the bridge with her child to escape the attack.

Ethan Hunt (Tom Cruise) runs towards the Tate, just behind the bridge, in *Mission: Impossible – Fallout* (2018) as he chases August Walker (Henry Cavill) who has a helicopter at the top of the museum's chimney waiting for him to make his escape.

Background
The Millennium Bridge is a footbridge spanning the Thames, connecting St Paul's Cathedral on its north bank to the Tate Modern and Shakespeare's Globe, on the south bank. The bridge was designed by Foster and Partners and Sir Anthony Caro and it was opened by Queen Elizabeth II in 2000. Just two days after opening, however, it was closed due to lateral vibration, leading to it being dubbed "the wobbly bridge", and when it reopened the numbers crossing it were limited. After two years of research, more than 80 dampers were added to solve the problem. Tate Modern, one of the world's largest modern and contemporary art galleries, opened in 2000 and is housed in the former Bankside Power

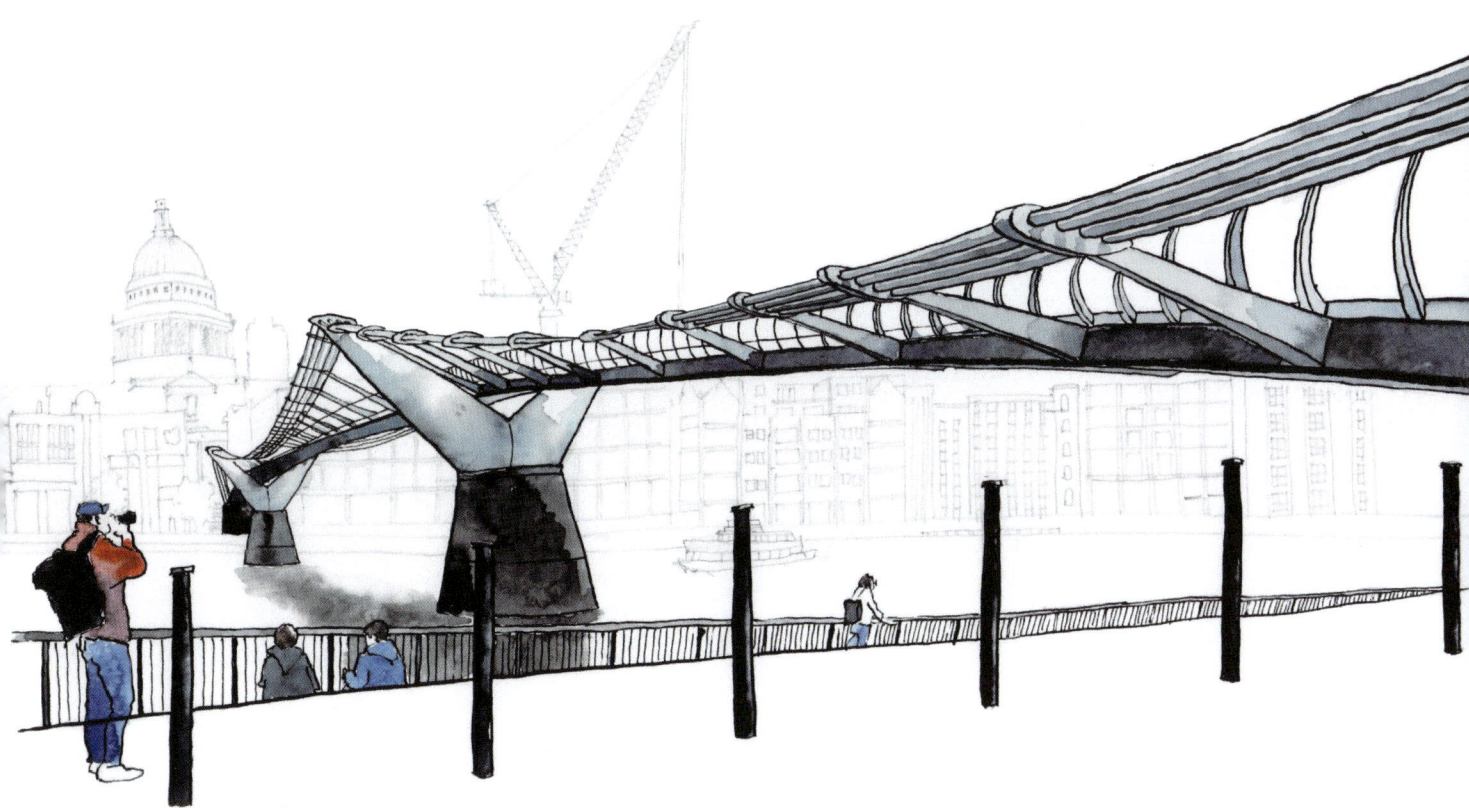

Station. Like many UK national galleries and museums, there is no admission charge for most of its areas. Also on the south side of the bridge is Shakespeare's Globe, a reconstruction of the Elizabethan playhouse where many of William Shakespeare's works were performed.

▶▶ *Continue your film journey to* **PARK STREET**

▸▸ THE WALKING GUIDE TO LONDON FILM SITES

LOCK STOCK AND TWO SMOKING BARRELS (1998)
15 Park Street SE1 9AB

Getting there
Continue in the same direction along the Thames Embankment from the Millennium Bridge, with the river on your left. Cross under Southwark Bridge and when you reach The Anchor pub turn right onto **Bank End**. Continue on **Park Street** when it merges from the right onto Bank End until you reach the railway bridge. Just under the bridge is number 15. *(journey time 10 mins)*

The plot
15 Park Street, a rundown, three-storey building with a peeling paint job and a boarded-up window, is the hideout of the film's main characters, a group of small-time East End criminals (Nick Moran, Jason Flemyng, Dexter Fletcher and Jason Statham). The gang attempt to pool money for a big poker game against a ruthless criminal, Hatchet Harry (PH Moriarty). The game is rigged and the gang end up owing the criminal kingpin a fortune.

Other starring roles
Near the beginning of *Entrapment* (1999), as a test, master thief Mac (Sean Connery) sends insurance investigator Gin (Catherine Zeta-Jones) to Haas Antiques, in Park Street, to steal a vase.

Park Street is also the location of the humble home of Leonard Bast (Samuel West) in the award-winning Merchant Ivory classic *Howards End* (1992).

Background
Southwark, the area surrounding Park Street, is the oldest part of South London and has numerous literary and theatrical connections. Many of William Shakespeare's plays were first performed at the Rose Theatre, which was located on the north side of Park Street. Charles Dickens, who grew up in the area, also set many of his novels, including *The Pickwick Papers*, *David Copperfield* and *Little Dorrit*, in Southwark.

▸▸ Continue your film journey towards **BOROUGH MARKET**

BRIDGET JONES' DIARY (2001)
The Globe Tavern, 8 Bedale Street SE1 9AL

Getting there
Continue along **Park Street** until you reach Borough Market. Turn right onto **Stoney Street** and walk to **Southwark Street** at the top of the road. Turn left and walk round the corner, where the road becomes **Borough High Street**. Turn down the first street on the left after that and the pub in **Bedale Street** is straight ahead. *(journey time 3 mins)*

The plot
Bridget Jones (Renée Zellweger) is a single woman who is trying to find love and happiness. She lives in a small flat above the Globe Tavern and she often goes to the pub to meet her friends. The area around the Globe is also where Bridget's boss Daniel Cleaver (Hugh Grant) and Mark Darcy (Colin Firth) come to blows during a birthday party.

Other starring roles
The Market Porter, a traditional English pub opposite Borough Market in Stoney Street, stood in for The Third Hand Book Emporium in *Harry Potter and the Prisoner of Azkaban* (2004).

The picturesque Thameside pub The Anchor in Bank End/ Park Street is where Ethan Hunt (Tom Cruise) has a drink with Luther Stickell (Ving Rhames) at the end of *Mission: Impossible* (1996).

Background
Borough Market has been a market for over 1,000 years. In the 19th century Borough Market became a major centre for the trade of meat and poultry due to its strategic position near the riverside and it continued as a mainly wholesale market until the late 20th century when it had begun to decline. In the mid 1990s the trustees took the decision to revive the area as a retail market and it has thrived ever since. Tragedy struck the Borough Market area in 2017 during the London Bridge terrorist attack when eight people were killed.

▶▶ *Continue your film journey to* **TOWER BRIDGE**

▶▶ THE WALKING GUIDE TO LONDON FILM SITES

SPIDER-MAN: FAR FROM HOME (2019)
Tower Bridge, Tower Bridge Road SE1 1LE

Getting there
Backtrack up **Bedale Street** to **Borough High Street**, turn left past the glass structure on the corner and under the railway bridge. Carry on towards London Bridge. Just before the bridge, cross to the other side and descend the steps on the right-hand side of the road at **No 1 London Bridge** to **Queen's Walk**, which runs along the riverside. Continue with the river to your left, passing the HMS Belfast, until you reach Tower Bridge. *(journey time 15 mins)*

The plot
Peter Parker (Tom Holland) is enjoying a European school field trip when he finds himself having to don his Spider-Man outfit to fight four elemental creatures, representing earth, air, water and fire. The climax of the film, where super villain Mysterio (Jake Gyllenhaal) battles Spider-Man, takes place on top of the famous London bridge.

Other starring roles
In the reboot of *Hellboy* (2019), Tower Bridge is destroyed by a giant demon which rampages through London. The bridge has also come under attack in a number of other films, from *Gorgo*, the 1961 feature about a British Godzilla, to *Independence Day: Resurgence* (2016).
In *The Mummy Returns* (2001) the heroes ride a double-decker bus across the bridge after being chased by mummies.

Background
The bridge, the first to cross the river near to the Tower of London, was officially opened in 1894 by the Prince and Princess of Wales. The high-level open-air walkways between the two towers were accessible to the public when it first opened but were closed in 1910 because they became the haunt of prostitutes and pickpockets and were seldom used by normal pedestrians. The walkways were reopened in 2014 when glass floors were installed, allowing visitors to look down at the river below. There is no truth in the urban legend that when American Robert Paxton McCulloch bought London Bridge from the City of London in 1967 for $2.4 million and rebuilt it in Arizona, he believed he was buying Tower Bridge. A guided tour of the bridge, including the walkway where Spider-Man battled Mysterio, is available to book.

▶▶ *Continue your film journey to* **GREENWICH**

▶▶ THE WALKING GUIDE TO LONDON FILM SITES

THOR: THE DARK WORLD (2013)
The Old Royal Naval College, Greenwich SE10 9NN

Getting there
Cross Tower Bridge on the left-hand side and descend the steps that appear on the far side on the left. Walk towards the Tower of London and follow the path to Tower Bridge Quay. Board the ferry bus for Greenwich Pier. Disembark at the pier and the Old Royal Naval College is directly in front. *(journey time 40 mins, excluding waiting time for ferry)* Alternatively cross the bridge and take the DLR from Tower Gateway to Limehouse and change for Cutty Sark Station.

The plot
The Royal Naval College at Greenwich is where the final battle between Thor (Chris Hemsworth) and Malekith (Christopher Eccleston) takes place, as Malekith lands his ship at the college and begins his attack designed to tear apart the universe.

Other starring roles
Empire movie magazine called the Royal Naval College "the most popular filming location in the world", with films as far back as **Indiscreet** (1958), with Cary Grant, being shot here.

Several scenes for **Pirates of the Caribbean: On Stranger Tides** (2011) were shot at the college, including the memorable chase sequence.

The college is used as a location for many of the scenes depicting the turmoil of the French Revolution in **Les Misérables** (2012), including the funeral of Lamarque and Javert (Russell Crowe) chasing Valjean (Hugh Jackson) and Cosette (Amanda Seyfried) on horseback.

Background
The Palace of Placentia, also known as Greenwich Palace, once stood where the Old Royal Naval College is now and was the

birthplace of Henry VIII and his daughters, Queen Mary I and Queen Elizabeth I. During the English Civil War in the 17th century the palace fell into disrepair and it was later demolished. The remains of the original palace can still be seen at the college today.

The current structure, designed by Sir Christopher Wren, was initially built as the Royal Hospital for Seamen and in 1806 thousands visited to see the coffin of Admiral Horatio Lord Nelson lying in state. Soon after the hospital closed in 1869, the site was converted into a training establishment for the British Royal Navy. It is now the centrepiece of Maritime Greenwich, a World Heritage Site described by UNESCO as the "finest and most dramatically sited architectural and landscape ensemble in the British Isles". Official tours of the locations are available on certain days.

▶▶ *Continue your film journey to* **RANGER'S HOUSE**

▶▶ THE WALKING GUIDE TO LONDON FILM SITES

BRIDGERTON (2020)
Ranger's House, Chesterfield Walk, Greenwich SE10 8QX

Getting there
From the front of the Royal Naval College, follow **King William Walk**, to the right of the college as you face it. Pass the Cutty Sark on your right and continue, crossing **Romney Road**, until you reach Greenwich Park. Enter through St Mary's Gate and follow the path on the right, always keeping to the right, up the steep hill until you reach the Rose Garden on your left. Ranger's House is opposite. *(journey time 20 mins)*

The plot
In the Netflix TV series, the home of the wealth Bridgerton family is located in the heart of London's Mayfair, however, in reality, the amazing wisteria-covered villa used for exterior shots is situated on the other side of London, in Greenwich. The central focus of the first season is on Daphne Bridgerton (Phoebe Dynevor), the eldest daughter of the family, and her entrance into the competitive marriage market, with many important scenes taking place at the house.

Other starring roles
Location filming in Greenwich Park led to Oscar winner Daniel Day-Lewis winning his first film role. Director John Schlesinger was looking for local children to be extras in a scene for **Sunday Bloody Sunday** (1971), starring Peter Finch and Glenda Jackson. Day-Lewis lived in Greenwich and was recommended to Schlesinger by a local shopkeeper.

Many period films have also been shot at Greenwich Park, including **Portrait of a Lady** (1996), starring Nicole Kidman, **Sense and Sensibility** (1995), starring Kate Winslet and Emma Thompson, and **The Secret Agent** (1996), with Bob Hoskins and Gérard Depardieu.

Background
Ranger's House is a Georgian mansion built in the early 18th century for naval officer Captain Francis Hosier. In the early 19th century, the house became the home of Augusta, sister of George

III, and later the official residence of the Ranger of Greenwich Park, a royal appointment with no official responsibilities. Today it is home to the Wernher Collection, a world-class art collection amassed by gold and diamond magnate Sir Julius Wernher around the turn of the 20th century. The collection is open to the public several days of the week.

▶▶ *Continue your film journey with a detour to* **THE O2 ARENA**

SUGGESTED DETOUR

The World is Not Enough (1999)
The O2 Arena, Peninsula Square SE10 0DX

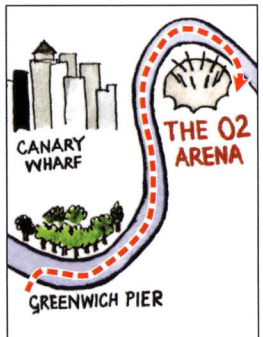

Getting there
From Ranger's House, backtrack to the Greenwich Pier. Take the ferry to North Greenwich Pier. It's then a short, signposted walk to the O2. *(journey time 26 mins, excluding waiting time for the ferry)* Alternatively take the DLR from Cutty Sark Station to Heron Quays, walk to Canary Wharf Jubilee Line Station and take the Tube to North Greenwich Station.

The plot
The O2 Arena features in the opening scene of the film. James Bond (Pierce Brosnan) is chasing Giulietta da Vinci (Maria Grazia Cucinotta) down the Thames. She attempts to escape by hot air balloon but Bond pursues her, clinging to a rope beneath the balloon. Eventually the balloon explodes killing da Vinci and Bond rolls down the roof of the the structure to safety.

Other starring roles
A TV movie *The Great Dome Robbery* (2002) tells the true story of the plan to steal the world's largest diamond from the Millennium Dome, as the O2 Arena was known at the time. The film stars Craig Fairbrass and tells how a gang planned to ram-raid the De Beers diamond exhibition being held in the Dome in 2000.

The location is also one of many London locations in the romantic comedy *Last Chance Harvey* (2008), starring Dustin Hoffman and Emma Thompson.

Background

The Millennium Dome was the original name of the O2 Arena, built to house an exhibition celebrating the beginning of the third millennium. The project was deemed a failure attracting around half of the 12 million visitors it was estimated would attend. Designed by the architect Richard Rogers, the Dome is one of the biggest structures of its type in the world, resembling a giant marquee, with twelve 100-metre high poles representing the months of the year or the hours on a clock face. The project closed in December of 2020 and five years later, in a deal worth £6 million, the Dome was renamed the O2 Arena. In 2007 it became a vast entertainment venue including an indoor arena, a music club, a cinema, an exhibition space, bars and restaurants. Bon Jovi played the first show in the new arena. The O2 isn't just an entertainment venue, however, visitors can also climb the roof guided by a professional climbing instructor to enjoy unrivalled views of the London skyline from 52 metres above ground level.

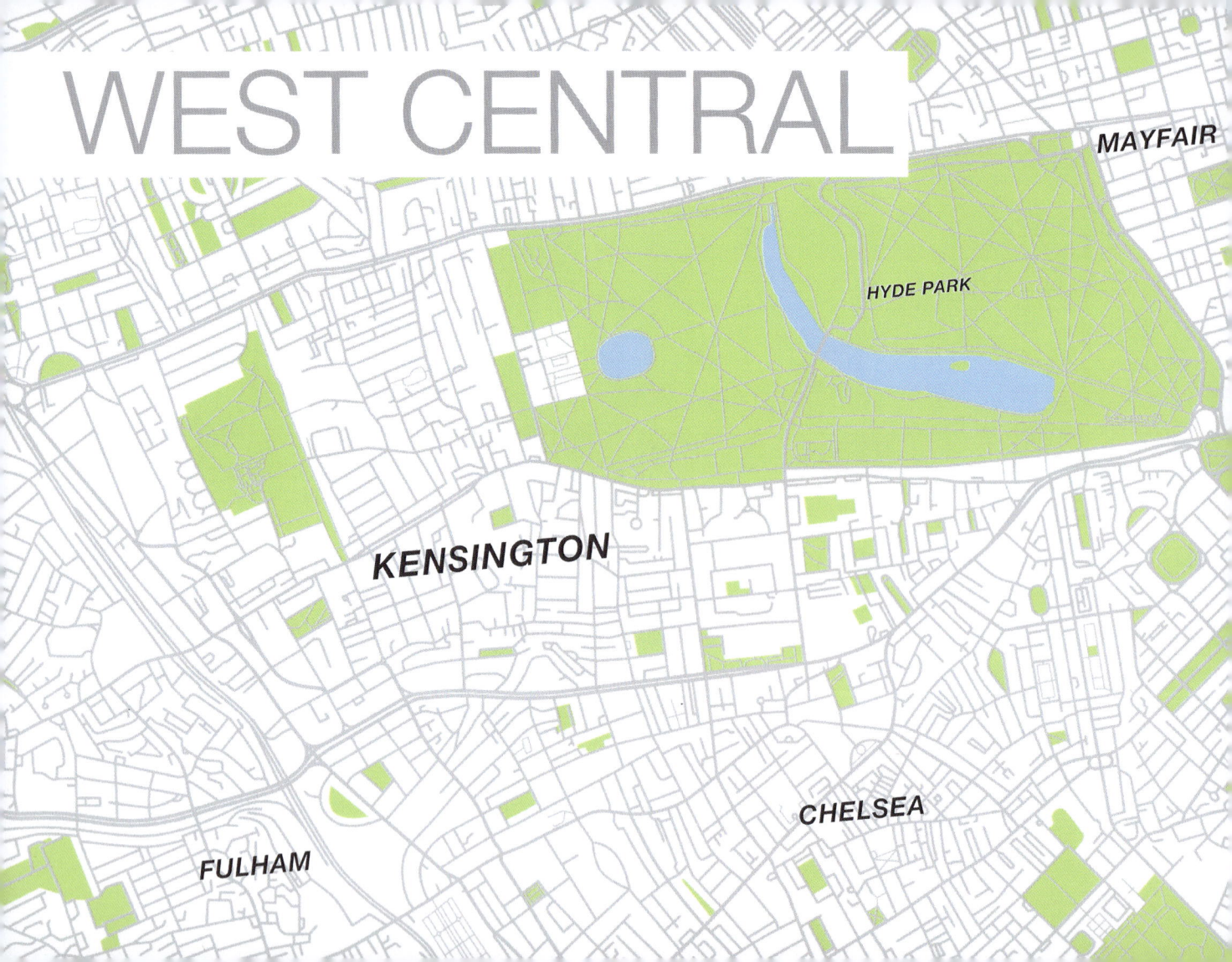

WEST CENTRAL

MAYFAIR

HYDE PARK

KENSINGTON

CHELSEA

FULHAM

SOHO

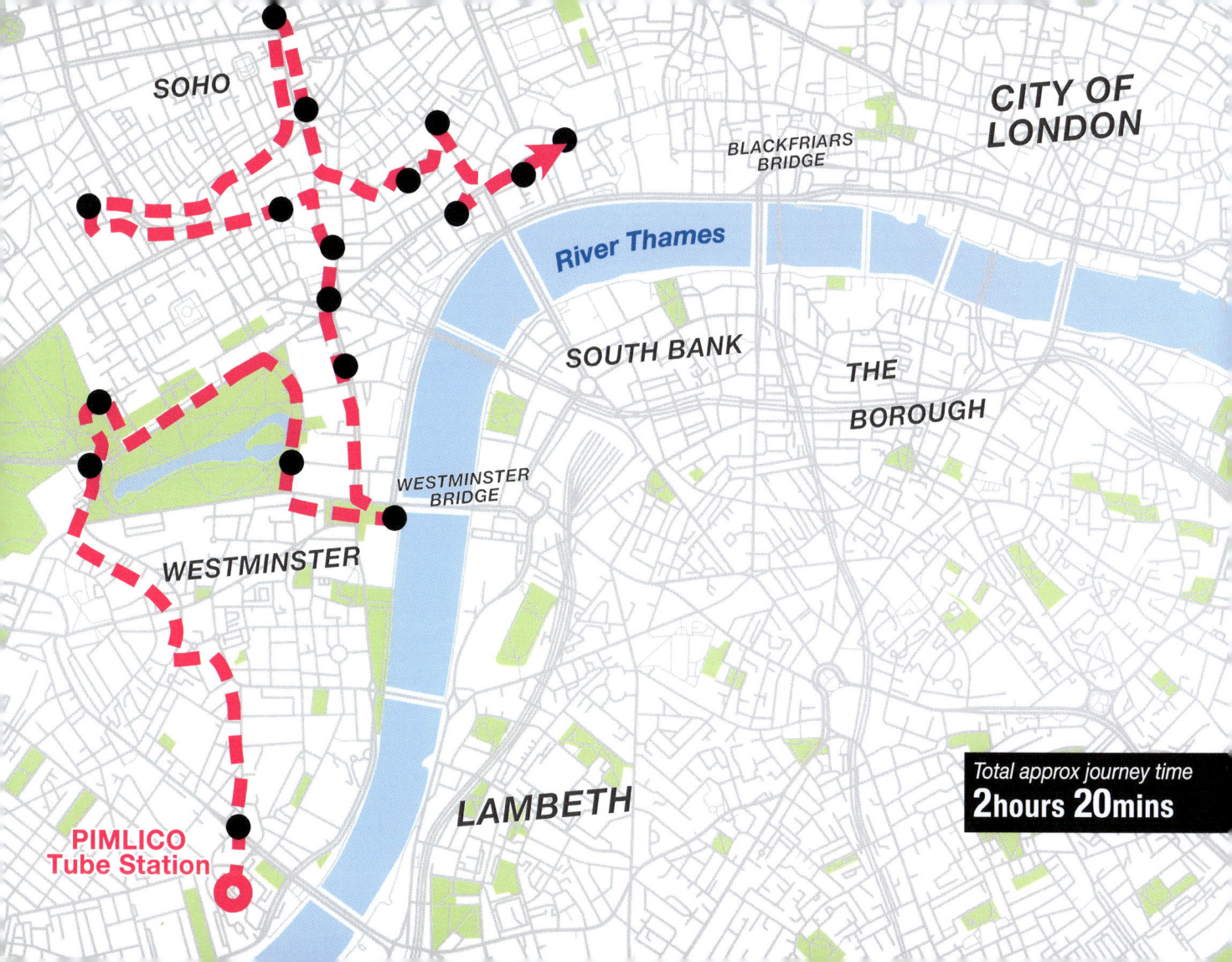

BLACKFRIARS
BRIDGE

CITY OF
LONDON

River Thames

SOUTH BANK

THE
BOROUGH

WESTMINSTER
BRIDGE

WESTMINSTER

LAMBETH

PIMLICO
Tube Station

Total approx journey time
2hours 20mins

▶▶ THE WALKING GUIDE TO LONDON FILM SITES

WEST CENTRAL

Embark on a trip through iconic landmarks in the heart of London, from the splendour of Buckingham Palace to the bustling energy of Covent Garden and the grandeur of Trafalgar Square, as we explore film locations that have thrilled cinema audiences worldwide

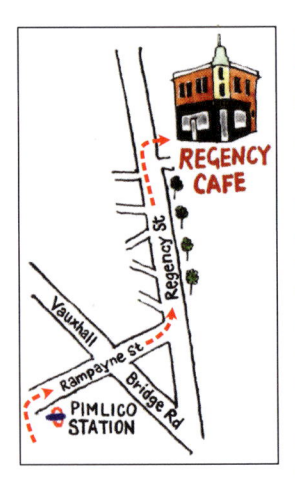

ROCKETMAN (2019)
Regency Cafe, 17-19 Regency Street SW1P 4BY

Getting there
Take the Tube to Pimlico Station. Exit the **Rampayne Street** entrance. Turn right and follow the street, crossing **Vauxhall Bridge Road**, until Rampayne Street meets **Regency Street**. Turn left and continue up the street, passing five side roads on your left. Just after **Fynes Street** you'll see the Regency Cafe on your right.
(journey time 7 mins)

The plot
The first meeting between Elton John (Taron Egerton) and long-term collaborator Bernie Taupin (Richard Madden) in the biopic was filmed at the Regency. The location stood in for the Lancaster Grill on Tottenham Court Road where the real meeting took place but which no longer exists.

Other starring roles
With its original interior tiling, the cafe has proved popular with film makers shooting period stories, such as the remake of the Graham Greene crime novel **Brighton Rock** (2010) set in the 1960s. Comedy-drama **Pride** (2014), which tells the story of gay and lesbian activists raising money for striking miners, is another period film shot at the cafe.

The memorable big fight scene in the crime thriller **Layer Cake** (2004), starring Daniel Craig and Tom Hardy, which ends with Freddie Hurst (Ivan Kaye) being burned with a teapot full of scolding hot tea, also took place at the Regency.

Background
The Art Deco Regency Cafe was established in 1946 as a cafe serving traditional British fare, catering primarily to local workers and residents in the Pimlico area of Westminster. The walls are lined by photos of famous boxers and Tottenham Hotspur memorabilia. The cafe's Full English breakfasts have received glowing reviews and renowned

Michelin-starred chef Michel Albert Roux has described it as his favourite cafe in London, a quote celebrated in a newspaper interview hanging on the wall of the restaurant. In 2013 it was voted the fifth best eating place in London by the website *Yelp*. Journalist Harry Wallop, writing for the *Daily Telegraph*, characterised the tea on offer as "Authentic builders' tea, reminiscent of the brew that once powered the bustling docks, factories and steelworks of Britain – a steaming cup of unadulterated, molten bronze." Try a cup!

▶▶ *Continue your film journey to* **BUCKINGHAM PALACE**

▶▶ THE WALKING GUIDE TO LONDON FILM SITES

DIE ANOTHER DAY (2002)
Buckingham Palace SW1A 1AA

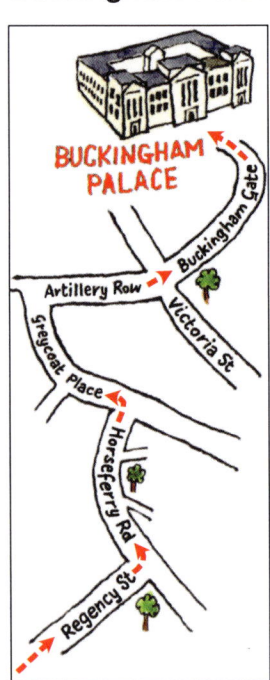

Getting there
Continue up **Regency Street** from the Regency Cafe until you meet **Horseferry Road**, opposite the Sacred Heart Church. Turn left onto **Horseferry Road** and follow it, past two streets on your right, until you meet a mini roundabout. Here turn left onto **Greycoat Place**, then right onto **Artillery Row**. Follow the Row, across **Victoria Street**, where it becomes **Buckingham Gate**, and continue on the road, past Westminster Chapel on your left. At the top of **Buckingham Gate**, you'll see the palace in front of you.
(journey time 16 mins)

The plot
In the film, as the media awaits the arrival of Gustav Graves (Toby Stephens) to receive his knighthood at Buckingham Palace, it appears the businessman is late for his appointment. With seconds to spare, however, Graves drops from the sky under a Union Jack parachute and lands just outside the palace gates with James Bond (Pierce Brosnan) watching on. Filming began as the sun rose at 6.30am and the area had to be cleaned up before 9.30am when preparations began for the Changing of the Guard.

Other starring roles
Many films have featured scenes filmed in and around Buckingham Palace, however, only a few have been authorised to film the actual exterior and no films have been shot inside the palace. The Royal Naval College at Greenwich has stood in for the royal residence in films such as *The Queen* (2006), starring Helen Mirren, and Netflix series *The Crown* (2016). Lancaster House, just five minutes from Buckingham Palace, is often used to stage interior scenes set at the palace and has appeared in many films, including *National Treasure: Book of Secrets* (2007) and *The King's Speech* (2010), and series such as *The Crown* (2016) and *Bridgerton* (2020).

Background
Built in 1703, Buckingham Palace has been the official London residence of British sovereigns since 1837, when Queen Victoria ascended the throne. The palace has a total of 775 rooms, including 19 State rooms, 52 Royal and guest bedrooms, 188 staff bedrooms, 92 offices and 78 bathrooms. Certain palace rooms are available to view on selected dates.

▶▶ *Continue your film journey to* **BRIDGEWATER HOUSE**

▶▶ THE WALKING GUIDE TO LONDON FILM SITES

DOWNTON ABBEY (2010)
Bridgewater House, 14 Cleveland Row, St James's SW1A 1DP

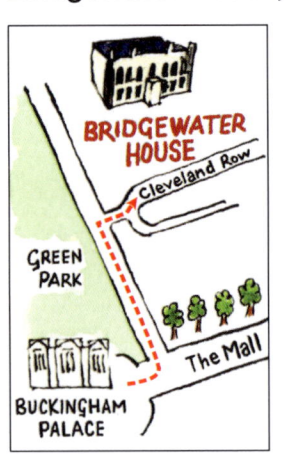

Getting there
From the front of Buckingham Palace, facing the Victoria Memorial, turn left and cross the road. Walk down **The Mall** away from the palace for a short distance on the left-hand side, past the pillar marked "S. Africa". Turn left down a small lane, lined with lampposts bordering the end of Green Park. Bridgewater House stands about 200 yards up the lane, through a small gate and lane on the right.
(journey time 10 min)

The plot
The house was used for the exterior scenes of Grantham House, the London residence of the Crawley family. It appeared in a number of episodes, with the family staying there for Rose's debutante ball and her wedding to Atticus. The interior shots of the Grantham House were filmed at Basildon Park in Berkshire.

Other starring roles
The house was used to shoot exterior shots of Marchmain House, an aristocratic palace owned by the Marchmain family in the classic 1980s TV adaptation of Evelyn Waugh's **Brideshead Revisited** (1981).

Nearby Lancaster House was once part of St James's Palace, so the building is another that is a popular location for British period dramas. Its interior has been a stand-in for Buckingham Palace in **Downton Abbey** itself, as well as **The Young Victoria** (2009), **The King's Speech** (2010) and a number of other films.

Background
Buildings on the current location of Bridgewater House have had a fascinating history, with the first being built around 1626 by Thomas Howard, Master of the Horse to Charles I and later the Earl of Berkshire. Later it was gifted to Barbara Villiers, Charles II notorious mistress and mother of five of his children. It is rumoured that he visited her at Bridgewater House via a tunnel from nearby St James's Palace. The house was occupied by the Parliamentarian troops during the English Civil War and also served as the Portuguese embassy for some time. The house sits in the St James's district of London, which was part of the gardens and parks of St James's Palace. It became a favourite location for the British aristocracy when it was developed for residential use in the 17th century and later became popular as the home of London's gentlemen's clubs.

▶▶ *Continue your film journey to* **CHURCHILL WAR ROOMS**

▶▶ THE WALKING GUIDE TO LONDON FILM SITES

DARKEST HOUR (2017)
Churchill War Rooms, King Charles Street SW1A 2AQ

Getting there
From **Cleveland Row**, walk back down the lane that borders Green Park until you come to **The Mall**. Cross the road, turn left, and follow **The Mall** to the end, then turn right into **Horse Guards Road**. Follow the road past **Horse Guards Parade** and the statue of Lord Mountbatten, past the gates at the end of **Downing Street**, until you reach a set of steps on your left, with a statue of Clive of India. The entrance to the War Rooms is beside the steps.
(journey time 16 mins)

The plot
Much of the action in the film takes place at the War Rooms, including the scene where Winston Churchill (Gary Oldman) delivers his first speech to the nation as Prime Minister in 1940. During that summer the news from France was bad and invasion appeared imminent, a situation he described in the speech as "a solemn hour". No filming was allowed at the actual War Rooms, however, so an exact copy was recreated for the film at Ealing Studios.

Other starring roles
The importance of the War Rooms in the outcome of World War Two is illustrated by the many films that have featured them, such as the TV movie *Into the Storm* (2009), starring Brendan Gleeson, and *Churchill* (2017), with Brian Cox in the titular role. Both of which also recreated the War Rooms in studios.

Background
Construction of the underground rooms began in 1938 and they became fully operational in August of the following year, just a week before Britain declared war on Germany. They were the main secret command centre for the British government throughout World War Two until the surrender of Japan six years later and were opened to the public in 1984. Churchill had an office-bedroom in the bunker, which included broadcasting equipment that allowed him to address the nation. To mitigate the health problems caused by spending prolonged periods underground, members of staff regularly used artificial sun lamps, a practice that often resulted in occurrences of sunburn. The War Rooms are open for visitors' tours.

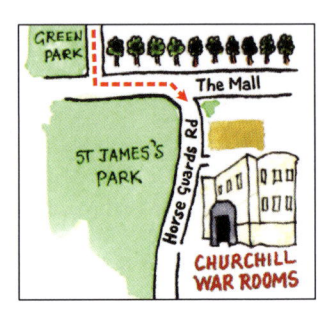

▶▶ *Continue your film journey to* **HOUSES OF PARLIMENT**

THE THIRTY NINE STEPS (1978)
Big Ben Clock Tower, 67 Bridge Street SW1A 2PW

Getting there
Continue along **Horse Guards Road** from the War Rooms until you reach **Birdcage Walk**. Turn left and continue as it becomes **Great George Street**, crossing **Parliament Street** at the traffic lights onto **Westminster Bridge Road**. The tower of Big Ben is on your right. *(journey time 7 mins)*

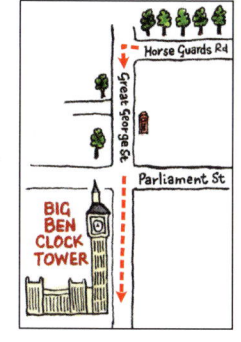

The plot
The Elizabeth Tower, to give it its correct name, plays a significant role in the plot of the 1978 film. Hero Richard Hannay (Robert Powell) discovers a secret plot designed to trigger war in Europe by planting a bomb in the clock tower intended to kill the visiting Greek prime minister. The bomb is set to explode at 11.45am and in order to stop the clock's minute hand reaching the IX numerals Hannay climbs out onto the face of the clock and jams the mechanism, allowing the safe deactivation of the bomb.

Other starring roles
As an iconic London landmark, Big Ben is often the target for destruction. Films where the Clock Tower has been damaged include Jack Nicholson's sci-fi comedy *Mars Attacks!* (1996), when it is targeted by aliens, and *London Has Fallen* (2016) starring Gerard Butler, in which a cargo ship explodes damaging the tower and killing the President of France.

Background
The Clock Tower, officially named the Elizabeth Tower in 2012, was constructed as part of the rebuilding of the Palace of Westminster after a fire destroyed the original structure in 1834. The bell inside the Clock Tower is known as the Great Bell, but it is commonly referred to as Big Ben. Each of the four clock faces is constructed using 324 pieces of pot opal glass, secured by a cast iron frame – a total of 1,292 individual pieces of glass. A guided tour of the Elizabeth Tower is available, however, tickets are limited and batches are released at regular intervals throughout the year.

▶▶ *Continue your film journey to* **WHITEHALL**

38

▸▸ THE WALKING GUIDE TO LONDON FILM SITES

OCTOPUSSY (1983)
Old War Office building SW1A 2EU

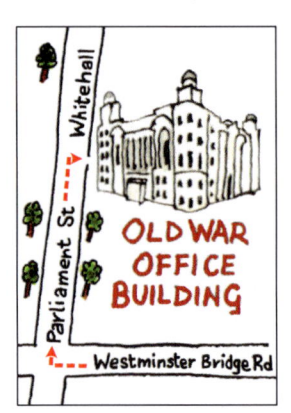

Getting there
Backtrack down **Westminster Bridge Road** and turn right onto **Parliament Street**, staying on the right-hand side of the road. As **Parliament Street** becomes **Whitehall**, continue past the Cenotaph war memorial and **Downing Street** on the other side of the road. The Old War Office is the next building after you pass the statue of the eighth Duke of Devonshire on the corner of **Horse Guards Avenue**.
(journey time 7 mins)

The plot
The first James Bond film to feature the Old War Office building was *Octopussy*, starring Roger Moore as 007, where it was seen as the headquarters of MI6, the British Secret Intelligence Service. The building's exterior was featured in an establishing shot, before the story continued inside the office of Miss Moneypenny (Lois Maxwell) and her assistant Penelope Smallbone (Michaela Clavell).

Other starring roles
After *Octopussy*, the Old War Office appeared in *A View to a Kill* (1985) and *Licence to Kill* (1989), again as the exterior of the MI6 headquarters. The building can also be seen in the final scene of *Skyfall* (2012), where Bond stands on a roof and looks out at the domed towers of the Old War Office building.

Background
The building was originally built to house the War Office, which was the British government department responsible for the armed forces. It took the place of the original War Office on the south side of Pall Mall, which had for many years been overcrowded, and its more than 1,000 rooms and two-and-a-half miles of corridors were completed in 1906. When the War Office was abolished in 1964, the building continued to be used by the Ministry of Defence until the beginning of the 21st century. More than 2,500 people worked in the building at its peak during World War One, including several hundred in specially erected huts that formed a fifth storey on the roof, referred to as the "Zeppelin Terrace" because of its vulnerability to German bombs. In December 2014, the building was bought by the Hinduja Group who announced plans to transform it into the UK's first Raffles Hotel.

▶▶ *Continue your film journey to* **TRAFALGAR SQUARE**

▶▶ THE WALKING GUIDE TO LONDON FILM SITES

V FOR VENDETTA (2005)
Trafalgar Square, London WC2N 5DS

Getting there
Continue up **Whitehall** from the Old War Office until you reach **Trafalgar Square** at the top of the street.
(journey time 5 mins)

The plot
A vigilante known only as V (Hugo Weaving) uses terrorist tactics to fight a fascist British government. At the climax of the film a tide of protestors, dressed as V, join his fight and begin to march from Trafalgar Square down Whitehall to the Houses of Parliament, as the military forces step aside.

Other starring roles
In *Wonder Woman* (2017) Diana (Gal Gadot) and the team attend the victory celebration in the square and mourn the loss of Steve Trevor (Chris Pine), while the nation celebrates another superhero's success in *Captain America: The First Avenger* (2011).

Canadian Prime Minister Robert Bowman (Nigel Whitmey) is assassinated when his car explodes driving by Trafalgar Square in *London Has Fallen* (2016).

Background
Opened to the public in May 1844, the square's name commemorates the Battle of Trafalgar, the British naval victory in the Napoleonic Wars. Charing Cross, the area around the square where six routes meet, has, however, been a prominent landmark for around 900 years, with the distance from Charing Cross being used as a location marker. Nelson's Column, built to commemorate Vice-Admiral Horatio Nelson's decisive victory at the battle over the combined French and Spanish navies, takes pride of place at the centre of the square. Other statues on plinths around the square are George IV and army officers Charles James Napier and Henry Havelock. A fourth plinth in the north-west corner of the square stood empty for more than 150 years and its fate was continually debated. Since 1999 a succession of art works has been commissioned for the fourth plinth.

SKYFALL (2012)
The National Gallery, Trafalgar Square WC2N 5DN

Getting there
You'll find the National Gallery behind Nelson's Column in Trafalgar Square.
(journey time 1 min)

The plot
In the film, James Bond (Daniel Craig) meets Q (Ben Wishaw, making his debut in the role) in front of *The Fighting Temeraire* by Joseph Mallord William Turner, in room 34 of the National Gallery on Trafalgar Square. After a short chat, Q passes Bond equipment for his mission and, as Q's predecessors liked to do, reminds him that he expects to receive it back in one piece.

Other starring roles
You can see Goya's portrait of the Duke of Wellington featured in the film *The Duke* (2020) if you visit room 45 of the gallery. The British comedy film tells the surprising true story of its theft by retired pensioner taxi driver Kempton Bunton (Jim Broadbent) in 1961.

In *Night at the Museum: Secret of the Tomb* (2014) the lions in Trafalgar Square come alive and confront a group including Robin Williams and Ben Stiller.

Background
The National Gallery was founded in 1824 and contains more than 2,300 paintings from such celebrated international artists as da Vinci, Titian, Cézanne, Monet, van Gogh, Michelangelo and Rembrandt, along with British painters like Turner, Gainsborough and Constable. The current building was opened in 1838 but over the years it has been added to in a piecemeal fashion, with only the entrance facing Trafalgar Square remaining unchanged.

▶▶ *Continue your film journey to* **THE GARRICK THEATRE**

▶▶ THE WALKING GUIDE TO LONDON FILM SITES

BATMAN BEGINS (2005)
Garrick Theatre, 2 Charing Cross Road, London WC2H 0HH

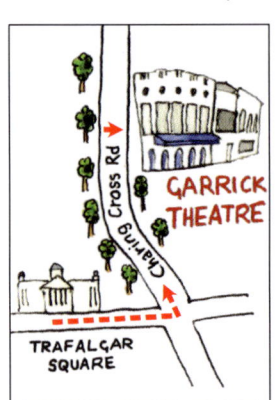

Getting there
Leave the National Gallery from the front entrance, facing **Trafalgar Square**. Turn left and immediately left again, past the National Portrait Gallery, and up **Charing Cross Road**. The Garrick Theatre is across the road on your right. *(journey time 2 mins)*

The plot
The theatre was used to represent the Gotham Opera House, where a young Bruce Wayne and his parents are attending a performance of the Italian opera Mefistofele. Bruce is scared by the bats on the stage and asks his father (Linus Roache) if they can go. After they leave the theatre, they are confronted by mugger Joe Chill (Richard Brake) and in the ensuing struggle both Thomas and his wife are killed. The events of that night set Bruce Wayne on a path that will lead to him becoming Batman.

Other starring roles
While the Garrick Theatre has not been used as a location for other films, London theatres have popped up in many productions.

The comedy murder mystery *See How They Run* (2022), for example, took place against the backdrop of the staging of Agatha Christie's play *The Mousetrap* and used several theatres for the filming. St Martin's in West Street features as the play's home in exterior shots, while The Ambassadors, next door, is the scene of much of the stage door action. On-stage filming took place at the Old Vic in the Cut on the South Bank and the Dominion in Tottenham Court Road stood in for scenes involving the front-of-house area.

In the Laurel and Hardy biopic *Stan and Ollie* (2018), a scene at the Glasgow Empire Theatre was filmed in the Fortune Theatre in Covent Garden, while in the film the Lyceum Theatre, also in Covent Garden, plays itself.

Background
The theatre, named after the famous 18th century stage actor David Garrick, was opened in 1889 and was financed by WS Gilbert, of Gilbert and Sullivan comic opera fame. It replaced an earlier theatre, also called the Garrick, that was demolished in 1881. Originally the current theatre had 800 seats on four levels, but the top gallery level has since been closed and the seating capacity reduced. When it opened it specialised in melodramas, but in recent years the theatre has mostly featured comedies.

▶▶ *Continue your film journey to* **SAVILE ROW**

ON ROUTE

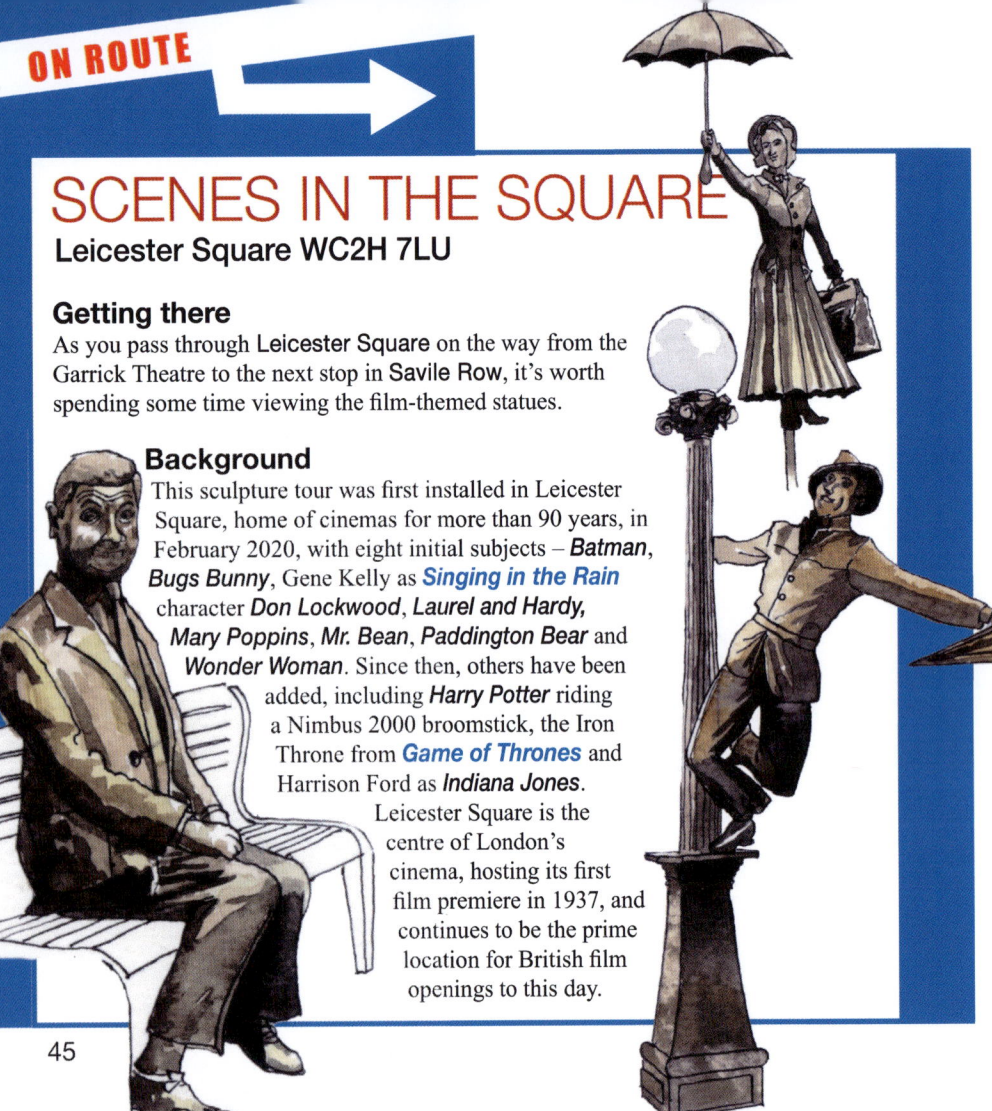

SCENES IN THE SQUARE
Leicester Square WC2H 7LU

Getting there
As you pass through **Leicester Square** on the way from the Garrick Theatre to the next stop in **Savile Row**, it's worth spending some time viewing the film-themed statues.

Background
This sculpture tour was first installed in Leicester Square, home of cinemas for more than 90 years, in February 2020, with eight initial subjects – *Batman*, *Bugs Bunny*, Gene Kelly as *Singing in the Rain* character *Don Lockwood*, *Laurel and Hardy*, *Mary Poppins*, *Mr. Bean*, *Paddington Bear* and *Wonder Woman*. Since then, others have been added, including **Harry Potter** riding a Nimbus 2000 broomstick, the Iron Throne from *Game of Thrones* and Harrison Ford as *Indiana Jones*. Leicester Square is the centre of London's cinema, hosting its first film premiere in 1937, and continues to be the prime location for British film openings to this day.

KINGSMAN:
The Secret Service (2014)
11 Savile Row W1S 3PS

Getting there
Crossing the road from the front of the Garrick Theatre, turn left and then immediately right to enter **Irving Street**. Continue along the short road and you'll reach **Leicester Square**. Cross the square diagonally leaving via the **Swiss Court** exit, past the Swiss Glockenspiel, and carry on along the right-hand side of **Coventry Street**, until you pass the entrance to Piccadilly Circus Tube Station on your left. Cross the road in front of you and continue up **Regent Street**. When you see **Vigo Street** on your left, cross the road and head down it. The first street on your right is **Savile Row**. Number 11 is a third of the way along. *(journey time 14 mins)*

The plot
Real-life tailor shop Huntsman plays the role of Kingsman, the

45

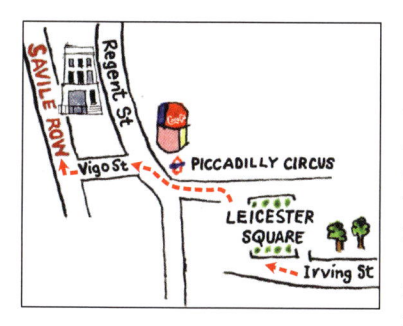

fictional premises in the film. After a secret agent, Lee Unwin (Jonno Davies), sacrifices himself to save his superior, Harry Hart (Colin Firth), the senior man feels he owes him a debt. Years later he meets Lee's son, Eggsy (Taron Egerton), and gives him a medal engraved with a phone number, explaining he should get in touch if he's ever in trouble. When Eggsy later contacts him, Harry explains he is a member of a private intelligence service that uses the Kingsman shop as a front.

Other starring roles

The headquarters of the Beatles' multimedia company Apple Corps was based at 3 Savile Row, where a studio was also built, and the group recorded their twelfth and final album *Let It Be*. The Beatles gave their final live performance, known as "the rooftop concert", on the roof of the building in January 1969. It was recorded for the documentary film *Let It Be* (1970).

Although in the early James Bond films 007 claims his suits come from Savile Row, the outfits worn by Sean Connery's character were actually made by tailor Anthony Sinclair in nearby Conduit Street.

Background

H. Huntsman & Sons, gaiter and breeches maker, was establishing in 1849 in Dover Street before later moving to Savile Row. During an appointment with his tailor, Huntsman customer and filmmaker Matthew Vaughn imagined what might exist beyond the walls of the fitting room, visualising the premises acting as a front for an organisation of spies, the Kingsmen. Famous Huntsman customers have included film stars, such as Rudolph Valentino, Clark Gable, Fred Astaire, Douglas Fairbanks Jr and Gregory Peck and royalty, including Edward VII and Queen Victoria.

▶▶ Continue your film journey to **CHARING CROSS ROAD**

▶▶ THE WALKING GUIDE TO LONDON FILM SITES

84 CHARING CROSS ROAD (1987)
84 Charing Cross Road, WC2H 8AA

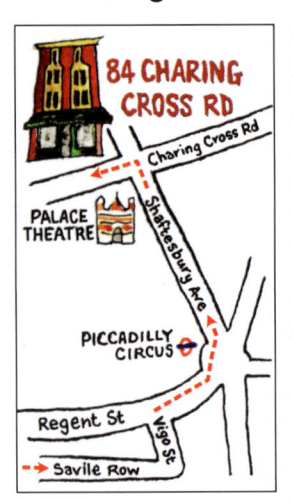

Getting there
From outside 11 **Savile Row**, backtrack and turn left back onto **Vigo Street**. At the end of **Vigo Street** turn right and follow **Regent Street** as it curves all the way down until it reaches the traffic lights at Piccadilly Circus. Cross over to the other side of the road and turn up **Shaftesbury Avenue**, the first main road on your left. Follow **Shaftesbury Avenue**, the heart of London's West End theatre district, all the way to the end. Turn left onto **Charing Cross Road** at the Palace Theatre. Just a short distance up on the other side of the road you will see **84 Charing Cross Road**, now a McDonald's restaurant, with a metal plaque commemorating the booksellers Marks & Co. *(journey time 14 min)*

The plot
Over a period of more than 20 years, through correspondence, a relationship grows between New Yorker Helene Hanff (Anne Bancroft) and a specialist bookseller Frank Doel (Anthony Hopkins) who owns a shop, Marks & Co, at 84 Charing Cross Road. Hanff plans to visit Doel's shop but for various reasons the trip is postponed. In early 1969, however, she receives the sad news that Hanff has died. The film tells the true story of the couple's friendship through a series of flashbacks and ends with Hanff's visit to the now closed bookshop in 1971.

Other starring roles
Harry Potter fans will recognise Charing Cross Road from **Harry Potter and the Half Blood Prince** (2009). As the Death Eaters attack London at the start of the film, they swoop down from the sky speeding past Trafalgar Square, along Charing Cross Road, and turn off the road into a narrow passage next to Great Newport Street, just yards short of 84 Charing Cross Road itself.

Another famous bookshop in Charing Cross Road, Foyles, appears in **The Guernsey Literary and Potato Peel Pie Society** (2018) as the venue for a book signing by writer Juliet Ashton (Lily James), who then heads to the island of Guernsey after receiving a letter from a member of the eponymous society.

You'll also find bookshops in Cecil Court, just off Charing Cross Road, appearing in many other films, such as **The Human**

▶▶ *Continue your film journey to* **TOTTENHAM COURT ROAD TUBE STATION**

Factor (1979), starring Richard Attenborough and Nicol Williamson, *Last Christmas* (2019), with Emma Thompson, and *Miss Potter* (2006), in which Beatrix Potter (Renée Zellweger) is shown how well *The Tale of Peter Rabbit* has sold when her agent (Ewan McGregor) takes her to a bookshop in Cecil Court.

Background

The former book shop is one of many that have closed over recent years and unfortunately now forms part of a McDonald's restaurant. There are, however, still a large number of specialist and second-hand book shops in the area. In the early 20th century, the area became famous for these shops with a huge number opening in both Charing Cross Road and nearby Cecil Court, which has itself hosted book sellers since the 18th century.

▶▶ THE WALKING GUIDE TO LONDON FILM SITES

AN AMERICAN WEREWOLF IN LONDON (1981)
Tottenham Court Road Tube Station, Oxford Street, London W1D 2DH

Getting there
From the front of **84 Charing Cross Road**, with the Palace Theatre on your left, continue up **Charing Cross Road** until you reach the junction with **Oxford Street**. Cross to the west side of the street at the traffic lights. The entrance to the Tube station is in front. *(journey time 6 mins)*

The plot
Two American backpackers, David Kessler (David Naughton) and Jack Goodman (Griffin Dunne), are trekking across the moors in Yorkshire when they are attacked by a vicious creature. Wakening in hospital David learns that he has been attacked by a werewolf. Tottenham Court Road Tube Station features when David moves to London and, transforming into a werewolf himself, he stalks a commuter waiting for a train on the Northern Line through the tunnels of the station before killing the man.

Other starring roles
The Tube network has been a popular location for major films over the years. Gwyneth Paltrow's famous life-changing **Sliding Doors** (1998) is one of the most memorable. The film of her journey was shot using a number of stations, but she first enters the Tube train at Waterloo on the eastbound platform of the Waterloo & City Line.

If you see a historic-looking station in a period film it's probably Aldwych on the Piccadilly Line, which closed in 1994 but continues to be used as a film location. It even has a train parked in the tunnel ready to film scenes. Such is the demand for filming on the network, London Underground has a dedicated department that deals with film requests, with an unused platform at East Finchley and the now redundant Jubilee Line platform at Charing Cross other popular locations.

Background
The London Underground station at Tottenham Court Road was opened in July 1900 as part of the Central London Railway, which now forms the central section of the current Central Line. Platforms for a second Tube line, the Charing Cross, Euston & Hampstead Railway, now the Northern Line, were added seven years later. Finally in early 2022 access to a third line, the Elizabeth Line, was opened. The station boasts a collection of colourful mosaics by Scottish Pop Artist Eduardo Paolozzi.

49

▶▶ *Continue your film journey to* **COVENT GARDEN**

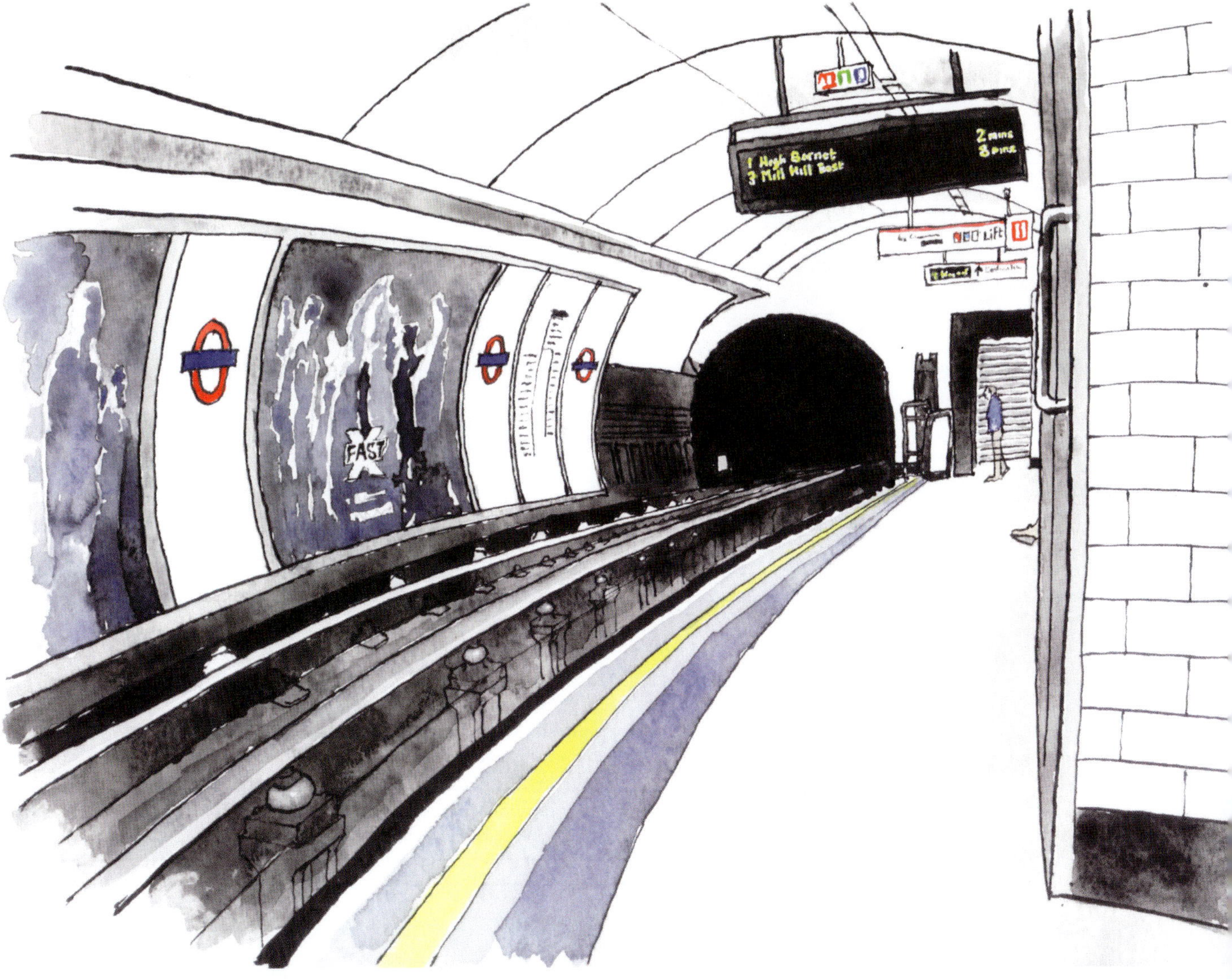
1 High Barnet
3 Mill Hill East
2 mins
8 mins
Lift
FAST

▶▶ THE WALKING GUIDE TO LONDON FILM SITES

MY FAIR LADY (1964)
St Paul's Church, Covent Garden, London WC2E 9ED

Getting there
Turn back down **Charing Cross Road** on the same side of the road you came up, past the Palace Theatre on your right and across **Cambridge Circus**, until you reach **Great Newport Street** on your left. Follow **Great Newport Street** until it meets a number of other roads. Cross diagonally to your right and follow **Garrick Street** until you reach **King Street**, third on your left. Head up **King Street** to the Covent Garden Piazza. The portico of St Paul's is on your right.
(journey time 14 mins)

The plot
Although the film was shot entirely at the Warner Bros Studio in Burbank, California, one of the best-known locations from the film, where Eliza Doolittle (Audrey Hepburn) sings *Wouldn't It Be Loverly* as she sells violets at the foot of the giant pillars of St Paul's, was filmed using an exact replica of the Covent Garden church exterior built in Hollywood. It's here that Henry Higgins (Rex Harrison), a professor of phonetics, first sees Eliza and bets fellow expert Colonel Hugh Pickering (Stanley Holloway) that he can change the speech of the cockney flower seller so she could pass as a duchess at an embassy ball.

Other starring roles
Alfred Hitchcock's penultimate film **Frenzy** (1972), a serial killer thriller starring Barry Foster, is set against the background of Covent Garden before the famous fruit and vegetable market became the shopping location it is today.

Emilia Clarke's character Kate in **Last Christmas** (2019) works as an elf in a year-round Christmas shop in Covent Garden. Don't spend too much time searching for it, however, as the shop front was a temporary build across a passageway between number 1 and 2 The Market and the interior scenes were shot entirely in a studio.

Background
The area where Eliza sang is, in fact, the rear of the famous old church. Access to the front is via the garden. The church was built in 1633 and, according to diarist Samuel Pepys, was the site of the first Punch and Judy performance. It has become known as the Actors' Church, with many famous thespians commemorated with memorials inside, including Charlie Chaplin, Noel Coward, Vivien Leigh, Ivor Novello and Boris Karloff.

▶▶ *Continue your film journey to* **THE ROYAL OPERA HOUSE**

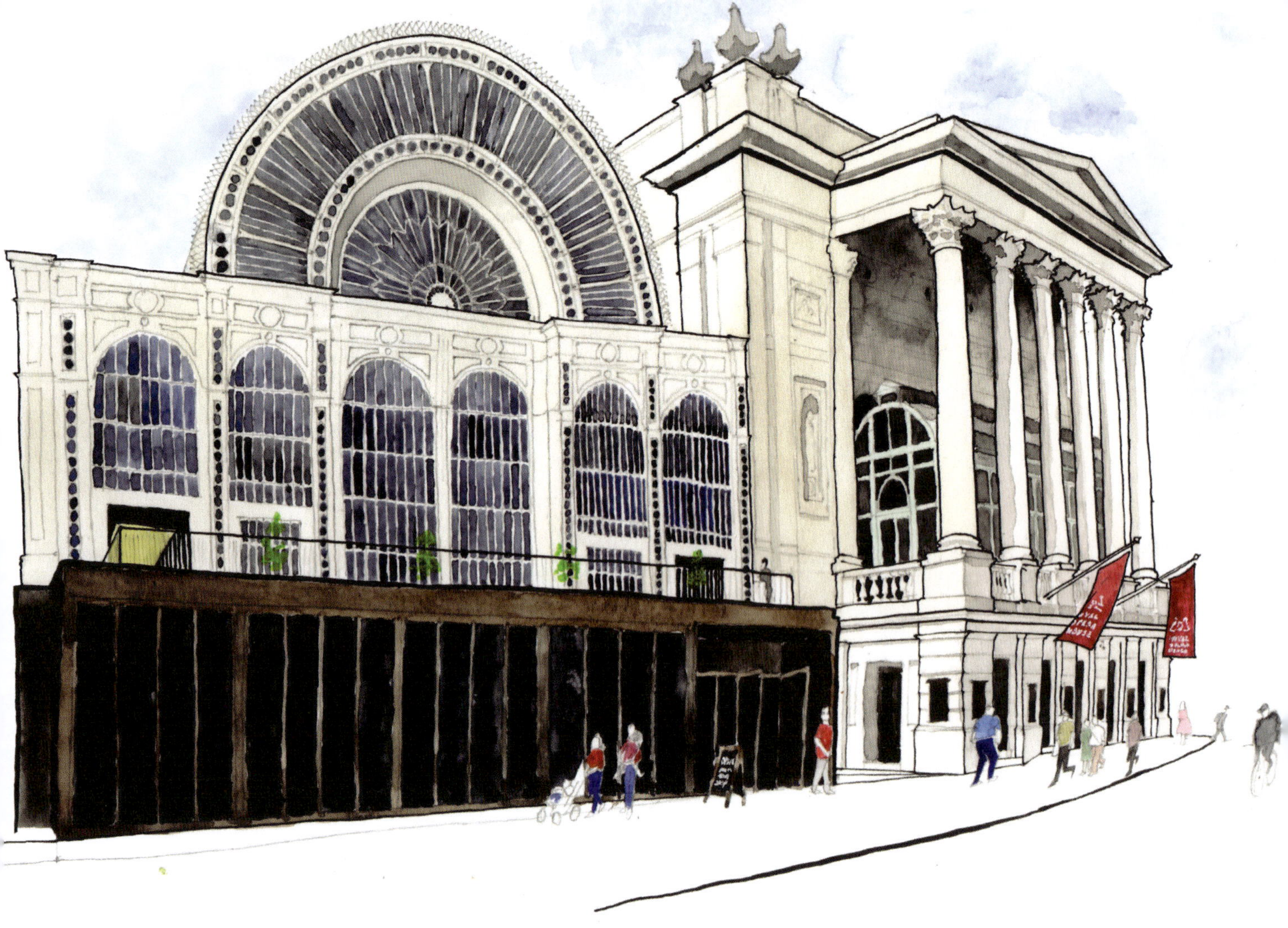

▶▶ THE WALKING GUIDE TO LONDON FILM SITES

THE FIFTH ELEMENT (1997)
The Royal Opera House, Bow St, London WC2E 9DD

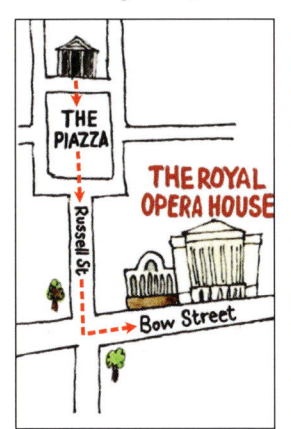

Getting there
From **Covent Garden Piazza** at the rear of St Paul's Church, walk straight through the middle of The Market itself until you come to a short road called **Russell Street** on the other side. At the end of **Russell Street**, turn left. The front entrance to the Royal Opera House is a short way up **Bow Street**. *(journey time 3 min)*

The plot
The Royal Opera House plays the part of a 23rd-century theatre in the classic Luc Besson film. Taxi driver, Korben Dallas (Bruce Willis) becomes involved in a search for a powerful weapon capable of defeating a great evil. Key elements of the weapon have been entrusted to an alien opera singer, Plavalaguna (Maïwenn Le Besco). In search of the elements, Dallas attends a concert at the theatre given by the singer but alien mercenaries, who are also on the trail of the weapon, stage an attack at the event and Plavalaguna is killed.

Other starring roles
The classic British film *The Red Shoes* (1948), starring Moira Shearer as a young ballet dancer torn between love and her career, opens at the Royal Opera House, which is home to Britain's largest ballet company, the Royal Ballet.

In *The Theory of Everything* (2014), the Stephen Hawking biopic, the theatre stands in for the opera house in Bayreuth, Germany, where the physicist (Eddie Redmayne) is watching a performance of Wagner's *The Ring Cycle* when he is taken ill and begins to cough up blood.

The opera house also has another film connection, having hosted the British Academy of Film and Television Arts awards (the British Oscars) from 2007 until 2016.

Background
There has been a theatre on the site since 1732 but the current opera house, the third after fires destroyed earlier buildings, was opened in 1858. Among many others, the theatres have hosted performances by the composer George Frideric Handel, the pantomime clown Joseph Grimaldi and the Shakespearean actor Edmund Kean. Ballet stars such as Margot Fonteyn and Rudolf Nureyev regularly graced the stage, as did opera singers including Tito Gobbi, Maria Callas, Luciano Pavarotti and Joan Sutherland. Guided tours of the interior of the opera house are available to book online.

▶▶ *Continue your film journey to* **THE SAVOY HOTEL**

▶▶ THE WALKING GUIDE TO LONDON FILM SITES

THE LONG GOOD FRIDAY (1980)
The Savoy Hotel, Strand, London WC2R 0EZ

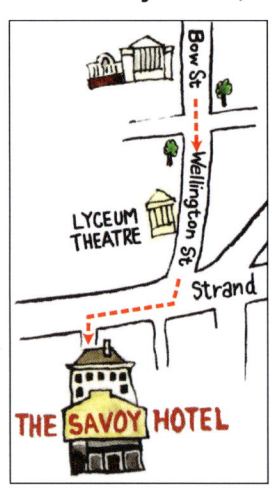

Getting there
From the front of the Royal Opera House, backtrack down **Bow Street** which turns into **Wellington Street**, passing **Russell Street** on your right, until you reach the bottom of the road at the junction with the **Strand**. Cross the **Strand** at the traffic lights and turn right. Pass **Strand Street** on your left and **Savoy Court** and the entrance to the hotel is the next on your left.
(journey time 6 mins)

The plot
The Savoy Hotel plays an important part in the story of London gangster Harold Shand's (Bob Hoskins) attempts to seal a crucial deal with an American organised crime group. At the climax of the film, as Shand leaves The Savoy, where the Americans have been staying, his car is commandeered by IRA assassins, including a very youthful Pierce Brosnan, who are about to wreak their revenge.

Other starring roles
The press conference scene from *Notting Hill* (1999), when Anna Scott (Julia Roberts) finally declared she would like to stay in Britain "indefinitely" to be with William Thacker (Hugh Grant), was shot in the hotel.

The plush interior of the luxury hotel also provided the backdrop to much of the action in the British comedy whodunit *See How They Run* (2022). *The French Lieutenant's Woman* (1981), *Entrapment* (1999), *National Treasure: Book of Secrets* (2007), *Stan and Ollie* (2018) and *Gambit* (2012) have also all featured the hotel.

The very first film to be shot on location at The Savoy was a silent adaptation of HG Wells' *Kipps* (1921) starring George K Arthur in the title role.

Background
The hotel was built by the theatre impresario Richard D'Oyly Carte, with much of the money coming from his successful Gilbert and Sullivan opera comic productions. Having experienced the opulence of American hotels during his trips to the United States, Carte decided to build the first purpose-built deluxe hotel in London. The Savoy was also the first building in Britain to be lit by electric lights, with electric lifts also installed throughout the building, along with the innovation of constant hot and cold running water. After Marconi invented a ship-to-shore radio transmitter, in 1905 The Savoy started

▶▶ *Continue your film journey to* **SOMERSET HOUSE**

advertising shipboard "Marconigrams", allowing travellers at sea to reserve a room at The Savoy before they even reached England. The hotel has been the London home for a huge number of famous guests, actors including Charlie Chaplin, Elizabeth Taylor, Marilyn Monroe and Humphrey Bogart, singers such as Frank Sinatra, Lena Horne and Judy Garland, and politicians including former President Harry Truman. British Prime Minister Winston Churchill regularly took his cabinet there for lunch.

Actress Vivien Leigh first met her future husband Laurence Olivier at the hotel and is said to have told her dinner companion that he was the man she was going to marry, despite both of them being married to other people at the time.

▶▶ THE WALKING GUIDE TO LONDON FILM SITES

GOLDENEYE (1995)
Somerset House, Strand WC2R 1LA

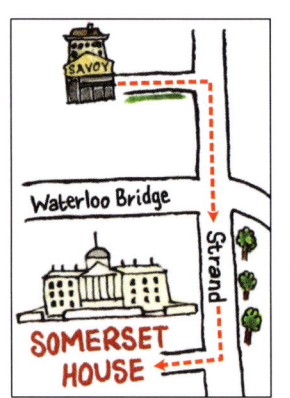

Getting there
Back track up Savoy Court and turn right onto the **Strand**. Continue along the **Strand** until you reach the traffic light crossing at the end of Waterloo Bridge. Cross over and continue along the **Strand** until just before St Mary le Strand Church appears in the centre of the road. Somerset House is on the right.
(journey time 5 mins)

The plot
In the film, James Bond (Pierce Brosnan) is sent to Russia to investigate a terrorist attack. Due to continuing political tensions in the 1990s, it was impossible to film extensively in Russia, so Somerset House stood in for a St Petersburg square where CIA operative Jack Wade (Joe Don Baker) breaks down after he picks 007 up at the airport. Production manager Crispin Reece explained the decision, "It looks imposing and authoritarian. It was a cold, grey April day when we filmed, so it was a shoo-in for Russia."

Other starring roles
Somerset House also appears in another Bond film *Tomorrow Never Dies* (1997) in a short clip of 007 (Brosnan again) driving into it in his Aston Martin DB5 for an MI6 meeting.

The building's neoclassical architecture has been used in many other films, however, especially period pieces. For example, it stands in for Manhattan at the turn of the 19th century in *Sleepy Hollow* (1999), starring Johnny Depp, plays World War Two British government buildings in the true story of *Operation Mincemeat* (2021), and is a 1960s Geneva bank in Marvel's *X-Men: First Class* (2011).

It also pops up as Oscar Wilde's (Stephen Fry) apartment in *Wilde* (1997) and in *The Duchess* (2008) as the Duke of Devonshire's (Ralph Fiennes) London home, Devonshire House.

Background
The house is built on the site of an old Tudor palace, with the current building beginning construction in 1776, and additions incorporated throughout the 19th century. The Registrar General of Births, Marriages and Deaths set up his office in Somerset House in 1837. This department held all birth, marriage and death certificates for England and Wales until 1970. In the late 20th century, Somerset House became the home of several art exhibitions, including the famous Courtauld Gallery.

▶▶ *Continue your film journey to* **AUSTRALIA HOUSE**

▶▶ THE WALKING GUIDE TO LONDON FILM SITES

HARRY POTTER AND THE PHILOSOPHER'S (SORCERER'S) STONE (2001)
Australia House, 71 Aldwych WC2B 4HN

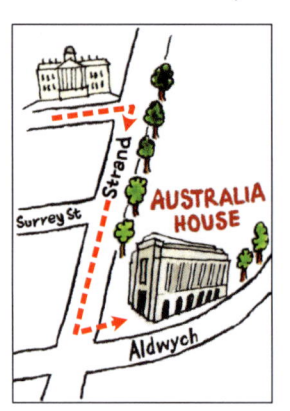

Getting there
Leave Somerset House by the main arch you entered through onto the **Strand** and turn right. Continue walking, crossing **Surrey Street**, until you reach **Arundel Street**. Turn left and cross the street just before **Arundel Street** and the main door of Australia House is in front of you. *(journey time 4 mins)*

The plot
The interior of Australia House was used as the location for Gringotts Bank, which plays a significant role in the film. When Harry and Hagrid go to make a withdrawal from Harry's parents' vault, Hagrid removes the Philosopher's Stone. The eccentrically angled exterior of Gringotts Bank is obviously a set, but the interior is the impressive Exhibition Hall of Australia House. When the bank appeared again in *Harry Potter and the Deadly Hallows Part 2* (2010) a replica of the Australia House interior was built at the film's Leavesden Studios, as the real Australia House wasn't suitable for the scenes involving dragons.

Other starring roles
Australia House has played the role of many imposing buildings over the years. The interior of the Cromwell & Griff auction house in *Sherlock Holmes: A Game of Shadows* (2011), where Irene Adler (Rachel McAdams) passes on a booby-trapped package, is another scene that was shot there, for example.

The same building was transformed into a London department store in *Wonder Woman* (2017), for a scene in which Diana (Gal Gadot) and Steve Trevor (Chris Pine) go shopping with Steve's secretary, Etta Candy (Lucy Davis).

While in another superhero movie, *X-Men: First Class* (2011), the marble-floored Exhibition Hall stands in for the Kremlin War Room in Moscow.

Background
When it's not acting as a film location, Australia House is the home of the High Commission of Australia, the country's diplomatic mission. Officially opened by King George V in a ceremony on 3 August 1918, the building was built over a 900-year-old sacred well drawing from the subterranean River Fleet, a major waterway in Roman and Anglo-Saxon times. Amazingly the well, now in the basement of the building, is still producing water fit to drink.

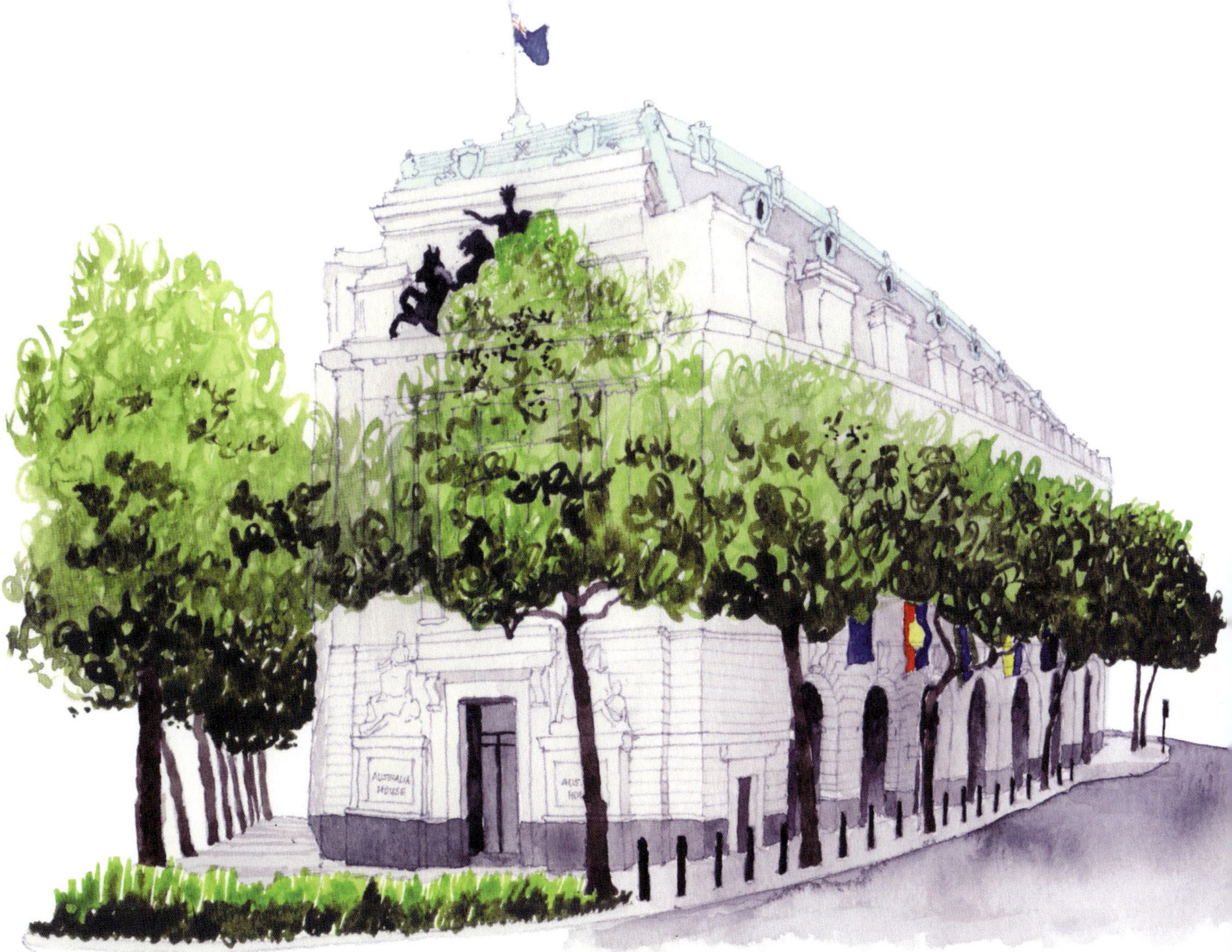
AUSTRALIA
HOUSE

EAST CENTRAL

SOHO

COVENT GARDEN

MAYFAIR

HYDE PARK

WESTMINSTER

SPITALFIELDS

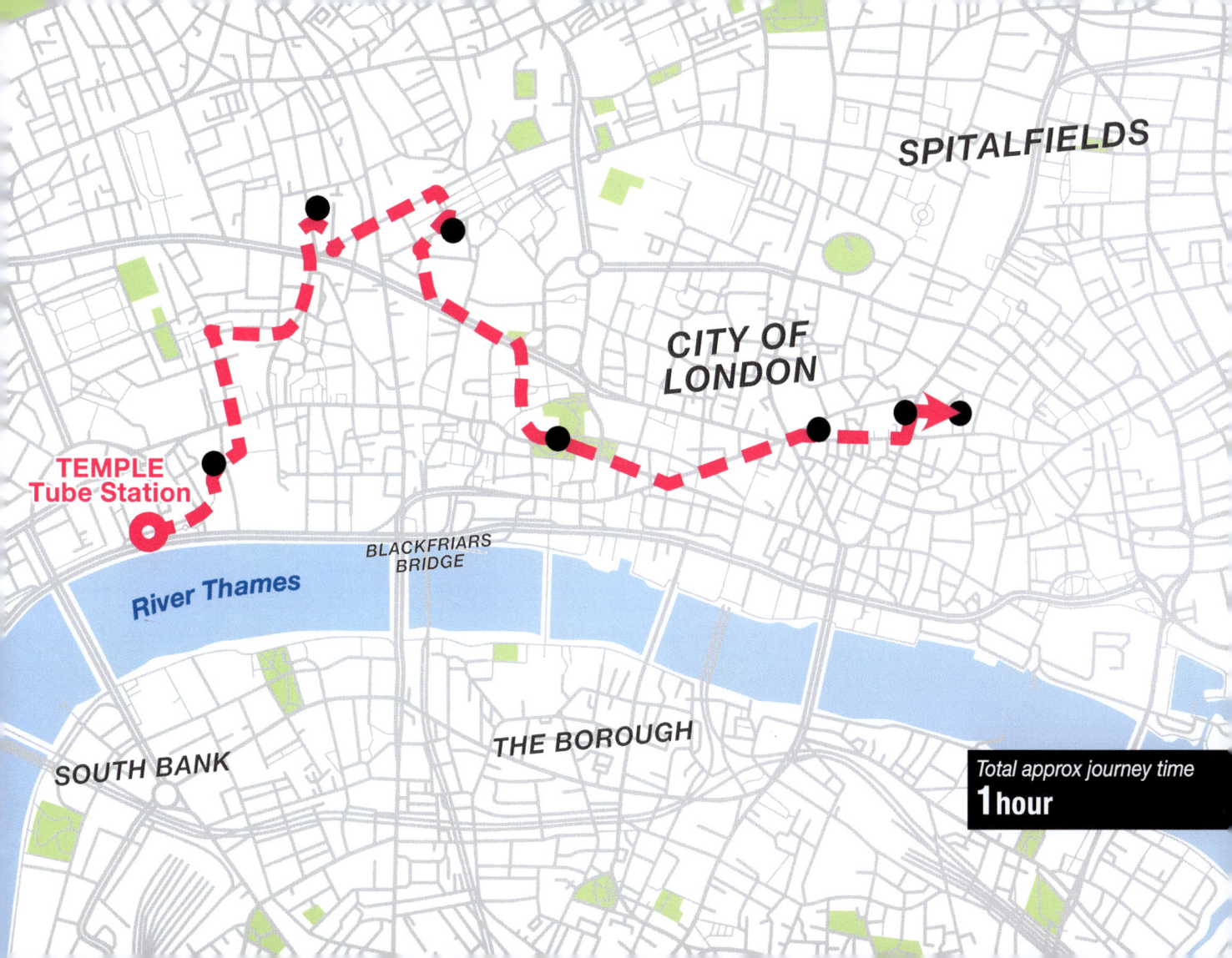

CITY OF LONDON

TEMPLE Tube Station

BLACKFRIARS BRIDGE

River Thames

SOUTH BANK

THE BOROUGH

Total approx journey time
1 hour

▶▶ THE WALKING GUIDE TO LONDON FILM SITES

EAST CENTRAL

Enjoy a short journey through London's favourite film locations as the gritty world of gangster movies, the enchantment of Mary Poppins and the romance of romcoms are brought to life

THE DA VINCI CODE (2006)

Temple Church, Temple, London EC4Y 7BB

Getting there
Start your journey by taking the train to Temple Tube Station. Exit the station and turn onto the **Victoria Embankment**. Turn left and continue, with Victoria Embankment Gardens on your left, across **Temple Place** until you reach the gated **Middle Temple Lane**. Turn up the lane until you reach **Pump Court** (there's a sign above the archway entrance) on your right near the top. Follow the lane and Temple Church is directly in front.
(journey time 6 mins)

The plot
In the film, Harvard symbologist Robert Langdon (Tom Hanks) discovers a trail of clues hidden in the works of Leonardo da Vinci that lead to the discovery of a religious mystery. Langdon heads to Temple Church to solve a clue involving a knight who was interred there. He finds a collection of stone statues of knights whose tombs lie in the church but soon realises the riddle is actually meant to lead him to Westminster Abbey and not Temple Church.

Other starring roles
In **Mission: Impossible – Rogue Nation** (2015), Ilsa Faust (Rebecca Ferguson) confronts Janik Vinter (Jens Hultén) in a vicious knife fight in the cloister of the Middle Temple, which looks out onto Temple Church.

In a more upbeat scene, Middle Temple is also the location where Jack (Lin-Manuel Miranda) sings *Trip a Little Light Fantastic* in **Mary Poppins Returns** (2018)

The buildings in and around Inner and Middle Temple have also featured in a huge number of legal and courtroom dramas on both TV and film.

Background
Temple Church is located within the Inner Temple, one of the four Inns of Court in London. It was founded by the Knights Templar, a medieval Christian military order established during the Crusades, who used it as their English headquarters, with construction beginning in the late 12th century.

▶▶ *Continue your film journey to* **YE OLDE MITRE**

63

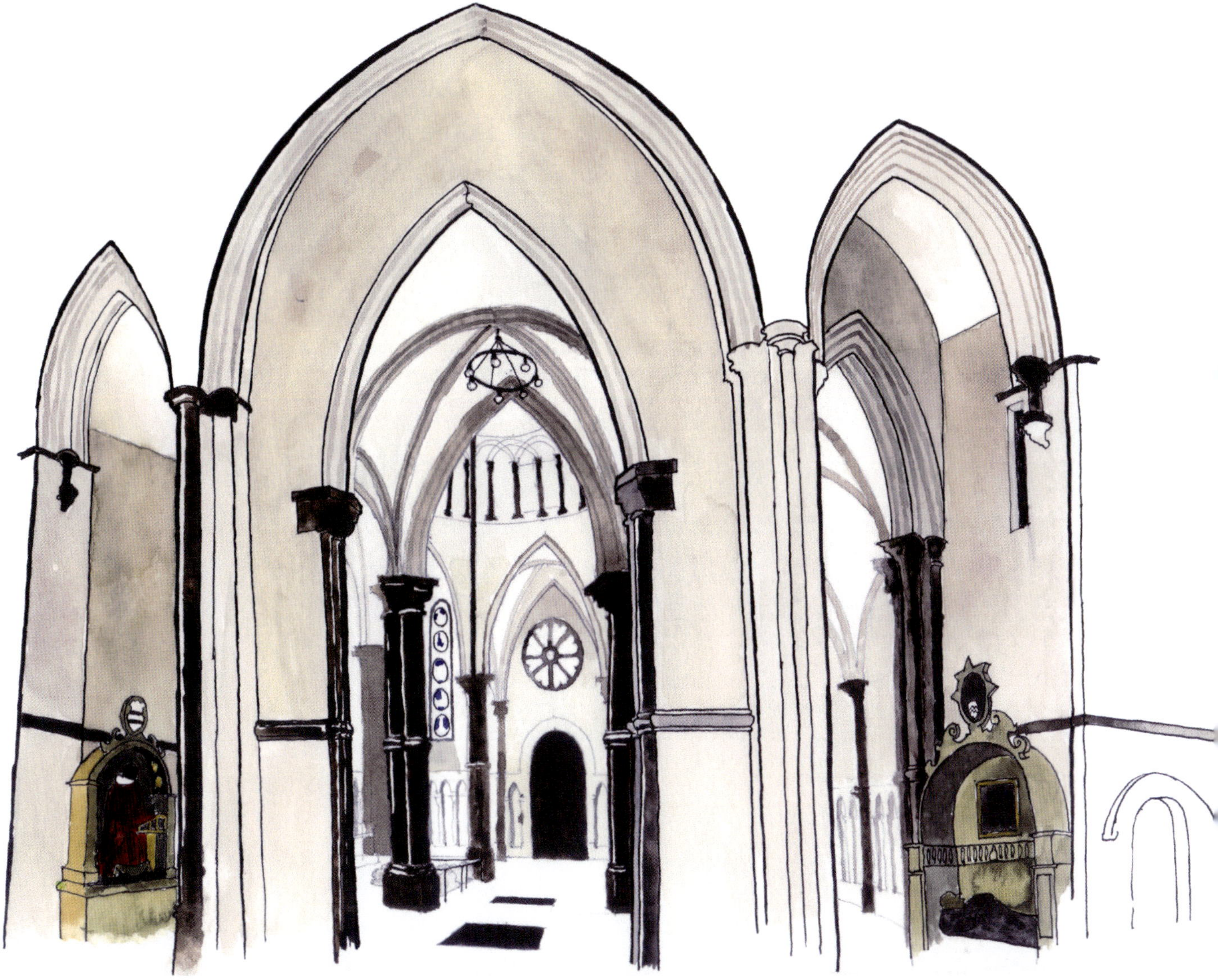

▶▶ THE WALKING GUIDE TO LONDON FILM SITES

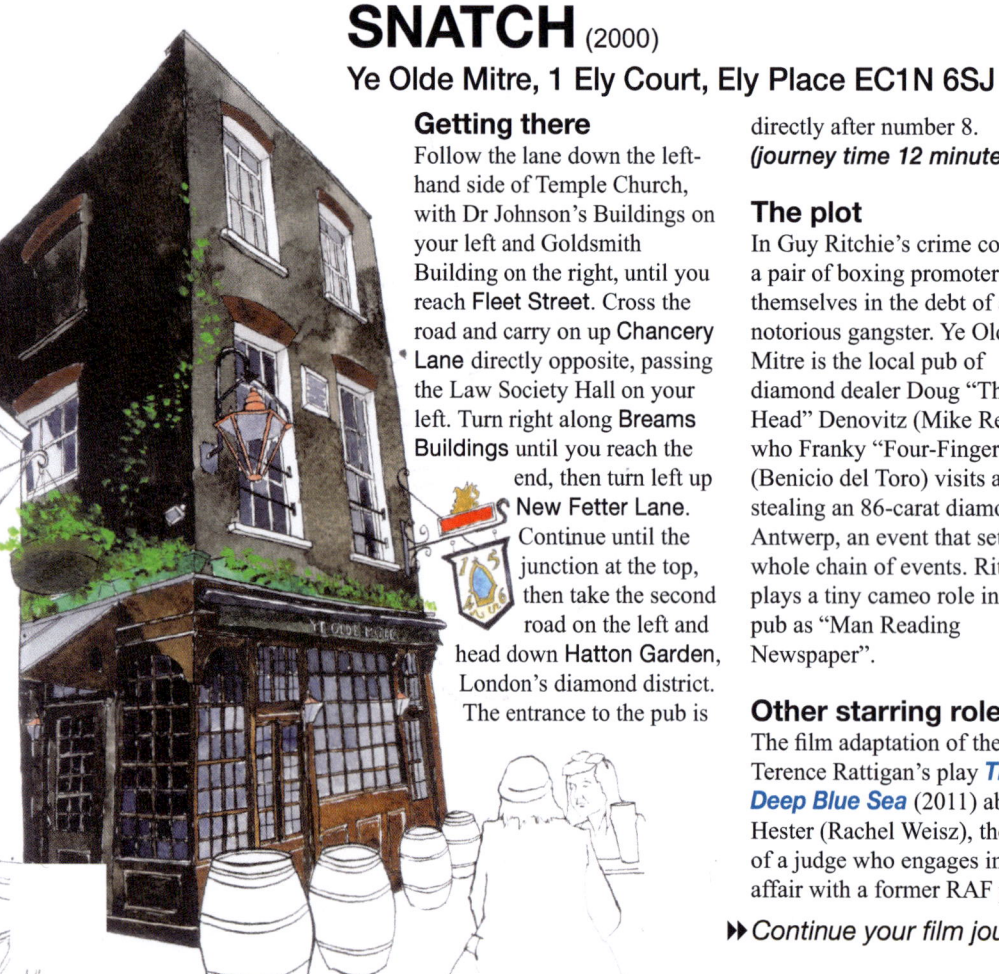

SNATCH (2000)
Ye Olde Mitre, 1 Ely Court, Ely Place EC1N 6SJ

Getting there
Follow the lane down the left-hand side of Temple Church, with Dr Johnson's Buildings on your left and Goldsmith Building on the right, until you reach **Fleet Street**. Cross the road and carry on up **Chancery Lane** directly opposite, passing the Law Society Hall on your left. Turn right along **Breams Buildings** until you reach the end, then turn left up **New Fetter Lane**. Continue until the junction at the top, then take the second road on the left and head down **Hatton Garden**, London's diamond district. The entrance to the pub is directly after number 8. *(journey time 12 minutes)*

The plot
In Guy Ritchie's crime comedy, a pair of boxing promoters find themselves in the debt of a notorious gangster. Ye Olde Mitre is the local pub of diamond dealer Doug "The Head" Denovitz (Mike Reid), who Franky "Four-Fingers" (Benicio del Toro) visits after stealing an 86-carat diamond in Antwerp, an event that sets of a whole chain of events. Ritchie plays a tiny cameo role in the pub as "Man Reading Newspaper".

Other starring roles
The film adaptation of the Terence Rattigan's play **The Deep Blue Sea** (2011) about Hester (Rachel Weisz), the wife of a judge who engages in an affair with a former RAF pilot, Freddie Page (Tom Hiddleston), includes a major argument between the lovers that takes place in the pub.

The jewel robbery in the comedy **A Fish Called Wanda** (1988) takes place in the Hatton Garden area, home to Ye Olde Mitre. Jamie Lee Curtis cases the joint at Diamond House, 38 Hatton Garden.

Background
Ye Olde Mitre dates back to the 16th century when Queen Elizabeth I is rumoured to have danced around a cherry tree in the garden with Sir Christopher Hatton, who was said by many to have been her lover. The stump of the tree can still be seen just inside the doorway.

▶▶ *Continue your film journey towards* **WEST SMITHFIELD**

FOUR WEDDINGS AND A FUNERAL (1994)

St Bartholomew the Great, West Smithfield, Barbican EC1A 9DS

Getting there
Back track down **Hatton Garden** from the entrance to Ye Olde Mitre and turn left at the bottom into **Charterhouse Street**. Continue up the road, crossing **Farringdon Street**, then passing **East Poultry Avenue** on your right until you come to **Grand Avenue**. Turn into **Grand Avenue**, which runs through the old Smithfield meat market, and cross the main road ahead. As the road curves round, the entrance to St Bartholomew is on your left.
(journey time 10 mins)

The plot
Over the course of five social occasions, a committed bachelor, Charles (Hugh Grant), begins to realise he's fallen in love with an attractive American, Carrie (Andie MacDowell). St Bartholomew is the church where Charles is due to marry an ex-girlfriend, Henrietta.

Other starring roles
The church features in a number of historical dramas. It stands in for the interior of Nottingham Cathedral in *Robin Hood: Prince of Thieves* (1991) and in Guy Ritchie's *Sherlock Holmes* (2009) is where Lord Blackwood is captured while preparing a human sacrifice.

The church also takes on a mythological nature when it appears as Thor's vision of Asgard in *Avengers: Age of Ultron* (2015).

Background
Barts the Great, as it is often known, was founded as an Augustinian priory in the first quarter of the 12th century at the same time as its neighbour St Bartholomew's Hospital. Its founder, Prior Rahere, ordered its construction after having a vision, while on a pilgrimage to Rome, instructing him to build a church and a hospital.

▶▶ *Continue your film journey to* **ST PAUL'S CATHEDRAL**

MARY POPPINS (1964)
St Paul's Cathedral, St Paul's Churchyard, London EC4M 8AD

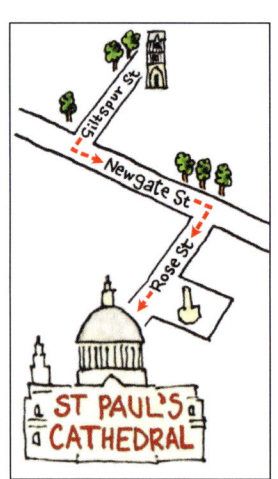

Getting there
Follow **West Smithfield** ahead of you when you exit St Barts and keep to the left as it becomes **Giltspur Street**. Head up the street until you get to a crossroads. Turn left onto **Newgate Street** and continue up the road until just before it forks. Turn down a small pedestrian road called **Rose Street** on the right. Continue along **Rose Street** as it becomes **Paternoster Square**, keeping to your right. St Paul's is directly in front. *(journey time 10 mins)*

The plot
One of the film's most memorable moments takes place when Mary Poppins (Julie Andrews), the magical nanny employed to look after the Banks children, sings the song *Feed the Birds* to the youngsters. Mary holds up a snow globe containing St Paul's Cathedral and the audience is transported inside the globe where an old woman sells bird feed for tuppence a bag. The film never visited London, however, and St Paul's was painstakingly recreated on a Burbank sound stage.

Other starring roles
As one of the most famous buildings in London, St Paul's Cathedral has appeared in many films. The real St Paul's appears in **Mary Poppins Returns** (2018) when lamplighter Jack (Lin-Manuel Miranda) cycles past the cathedral, where the bird lady is still selling her wares.

In **Mission: Impossible – Fallout** (2018), Ethan Hunt (Tom Cruise) runs into the cathedral during a funeral to escape pursuit and is chased up the stunning Dean's Stairs to the dome where he leaps to a nearby building.

An anomaly transports Thor and the evil Malekith to Earth in **Thor: The Dark World** (2013), where they arrive at St Paul's Cathedral.

Background
The first church on the site of St Paul's was founded in 604 AD. Two further cathedrals are believed to have been built on the same spot before construction began on a fourth St Paul's in 1087. This stood for nearly 600 years, before it was destroyed in 1666's Great Fire of London. The current cathedral was started in 1675 and took more than 35 years to complete. In July 1981, the cathedral hosted the wedding of Prince Charles and Lady Diana Spencer. It was chosen as the venue rather than Westminster Abbey, traditionally the site of royal weddings, because the cathedral offered more seating.

▶▶ *Continue your film journey to* **THE ROYAL EXCHANGE**

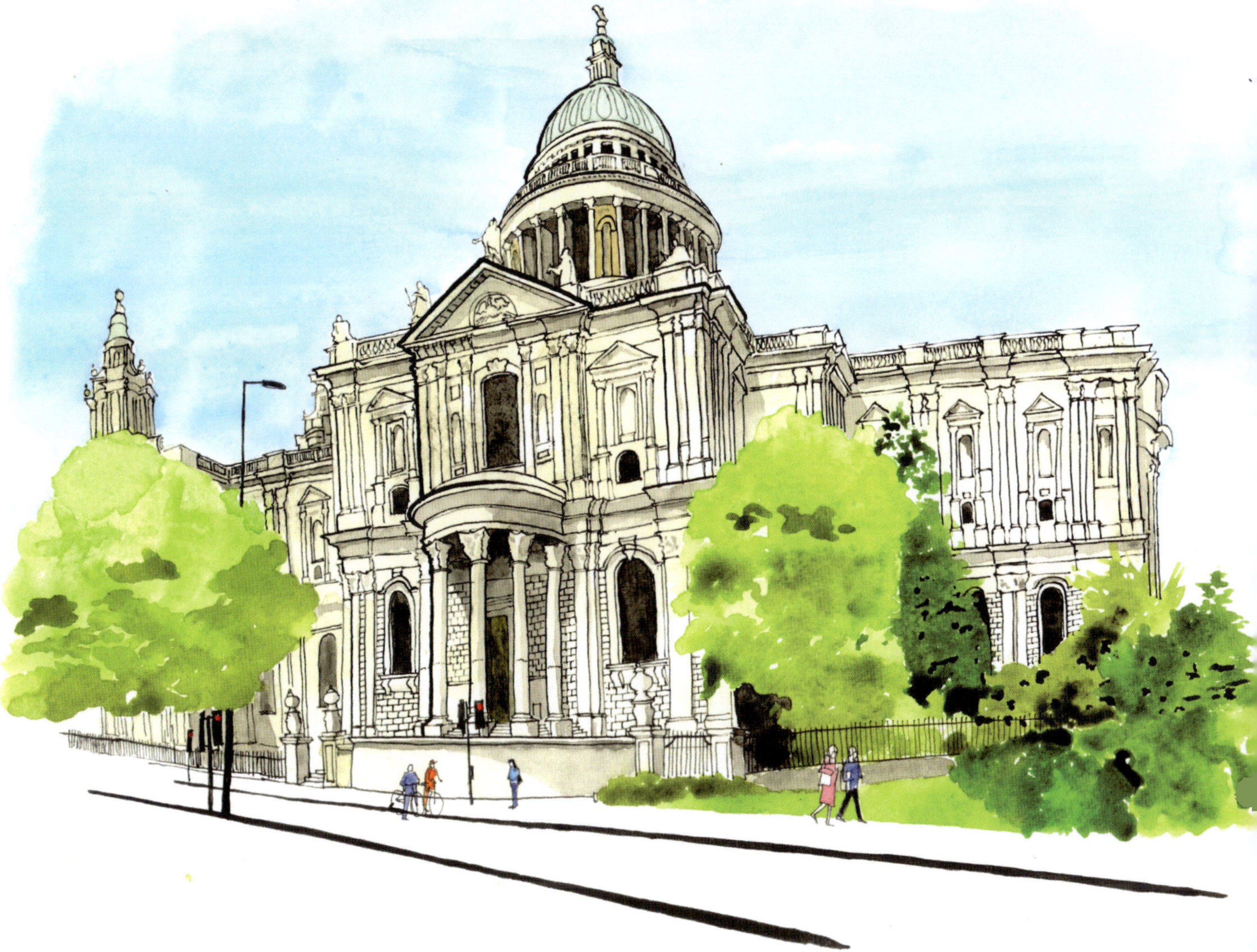

▶▶ THE WALKING GUIDE TO LONDON FILM SITES

MARY POPPINS RETURNS (2018)
The Royal Exchange, EC3V 3LP

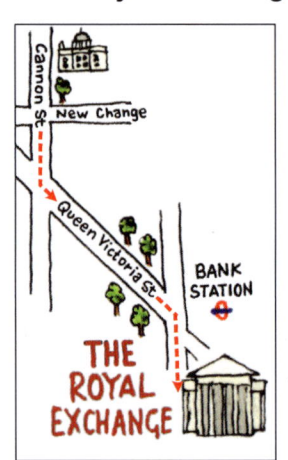

Getting there
From Paternoster Square, turn right past the West Entrance of the St Paul's, then turn left and walk past the front of the cathedral along **St Paul's Churchyard**. Passing **Festival Gardens** on your left, as the road becomes **Cannon Street**, continue across **New Change**. Follow the street until the junction and turn left along **Queen Victoria Street**. At the end of the street, cross the road and turn right into **Mansion House Street**. The Royal Exchange, with its statue of Wellington, is ahead of you where the street forks.
(journey time 14 mins)

The plot
The classical pillared frontage of the Fidelity Fiduciary Bank in the film is that of the old Royal Exchange Buildings. It's here that Michael Banks (Ben Whishaw) and his sister Jane (Emily Mortimer), the two children cared for by Mary Poppins in the 1964 original, go to retrieve shares in the bank he believes will allow him to repay an outstanding loan that if unsettled will see his house repossessed.

Other starring roles
The climax of **Bridget Jones's Diary** (2001), when Bridget (Renée Zellweger) and Mark (Colin Firth) kiss in the snow, was filmed at the Royal Exchange, even though in the film it appears the couple are just a few seconds away from her room at the Globe in Borough Market.

The Cornhill district where the Royal Exchange is situated stood in for London's West End shopping area in the scene from **Suffragette** (2015) in which Maud (Carey Mulligan) is shocked as the windows of an upmarket store are smashed.

Background
The Royal Exchange was founded in the 16th century by a merchant, Sir Thomas Gresham, to act as the City of London's first purpose-built centre for trading stocks. Two storeys were added to the original trading floor in the mid-17th century to house retail businesses, but, like much of the surrounding area, the original Royal Exchange was destroyed by the Great Fire of London. This led to a second complex being built and opened in 1669, however, this too burned down when a stove overturned in 1838. A third building, opened in 1844, is the one that still stands today. It was totally renovated as a luxury shopping and dining centre at the start of the 21st century.

▶▶ Continue your film journey to **LEADENHALL MARKET**

ANNO · ELIZABETHAE · R · XIII · CONDITVM · ANNO · VICTORIAE · R · XIII · RESTAVRATVM
WELLINGTON

HARRY POTTER AND THE PHILOSOPHER'S (SORCERER'S) STONE (2001)
Leadenhall Market, Bull's Head Passage, off Gracechurch Street, London EC3V 1LU

Getting there
Facing the front of the Royal Exchange, take **Cornhill** that runs down the right-hand side. At the crossroads, turn right into **Gracechurch Street** and Leadenhall Market is 50 yards on the left. Enter the Market, then turn right and then second right to find **Bull's Head Passage.**
(journey time 6 mins)

The plot
Harry and Hagrid walk through Leadenhall Market near the beginning of the first film, heading towards the Leaky Cauldron and Diagon Alley. Harry reads out a list of requirements for Hogwarts: "All student must be equipped with one standard size 2 pewter cauldron and may bring if they desire an owl, a cat or a toad." He asks Hagrid if he can find all these things in London and Hagrid replies, "If you know where to go". They turn right, down a small street, and through a door into the Leaky Cauldron. The door has been repainted, but you can still see the unmistakeable shape of the entrance in Bull's Head Passage.

Other starring roles
In *Lara Croft: Tomb Raider* (2001) Lara (Angelina Jolie) races through Leadenhall Market on her bike as she returns from the auction house.

The restyled magic show run by Christopher Plummer's eponymous character in Terry Gilliam's *The Imaginarium of Dr Parnassus* (2009) is a huge hit when it makes its debut at the Leadenhall Market.

Hollywood legend John Wayne, playing a Chicago cop sent to London, in *Brannigan* (1975) is involved in a bar room brawl in Leadenhall's 18th century pub the Lamb Tavern.

Background

Leadenhall Market has a long and celebrated history dating back to the 14th century. Originally built as a place for merchants to sell meat, poultry and game, it was also used as a granary and a storage facility. Long before that, however, the Market stood at the centre of Roman Londinium and below its cobblestones still lie the remains of the Roman forum and courts. By 1600 it had become the most important market in London. The medieval street plan was kept when the market was rebuilt in the 19th century, allowing current visitors a similar experience to that of their medieval predecessors.

▶▶ Continue your film journey to
THE LLOYD'S BUILDING

▶▶ THE WALKING GUIDE TO LONDON FILM SITES

GUARDIANS OF THE GALAXY (2014)
The Lloyd's building, London EC3V 1LR

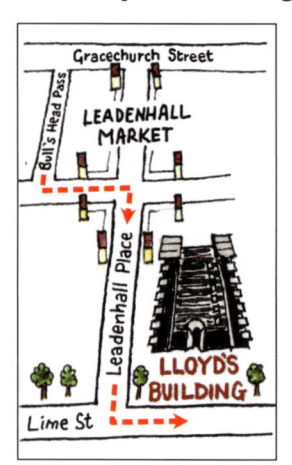

Getting there
Walk straight through Leadenhall Market from the Gracechurch Street entrance to the Leadenhall Place entrance. On your left is the Lloyd's Building. Turn left to reach the front of the building where the scenes were filmed. *[journey time 2 mins]*

The plot
The building's polished metal exterior staircases play the part of the city of Xandar during the attack by Ronan the Accuser (Lee Pace). The Battle of Xandar took place at the height of the Kree-Nova War, when Ronan the Accuser launched an onslaught on the planet using his entire army of Sakaarans to bomb it.

Other starring roles
The film version of the cult TV series **The Avengers** (1998) sees Emma Peel (Uma Thurman) comes face to face with her evil clone outside the building.

In the action movie **Entrapment** (1999) the building, which is owned by the British insurance giant Lloyd's of London, plays the New York headquarters of another insurance company, Waverly, the firm investigator Virginia (Catherine Zeta-Jones) works for.

The building has also appeared in a host of other films, including the Abba movie **Mamma Mia!** (2008), sci-fi drama **Code 46** (2003) and even cult classic **Trainspotting** (1996).

Background
The building is the home of the insurance institution Lloyd's of London and the business first moved to the site in 1928. As a company, Lloyd's dates back to the 17th century, when it was formed by Edward Lloyd in Lloyd's Coffee House. As the business was frequented by sailors, merchants and ship owners it became known as an ideal place to gain marine insurance. The company had several homes before moving to Leadenhall Street in the 1920s and continued to grow, expanding to a second building in Lime Street in 1958. When it outgrew the two sites it was agreed that the Leadenhall offices should be demolished and a new headquarters erected. The company ran an competition to find a design for the new building, won by the architect Richard Rogers. Like his design for the Pompidou Centre in Paris, all the services – like lifts, pipes and staircases – are on the outside, leaving the interior uncluttered.

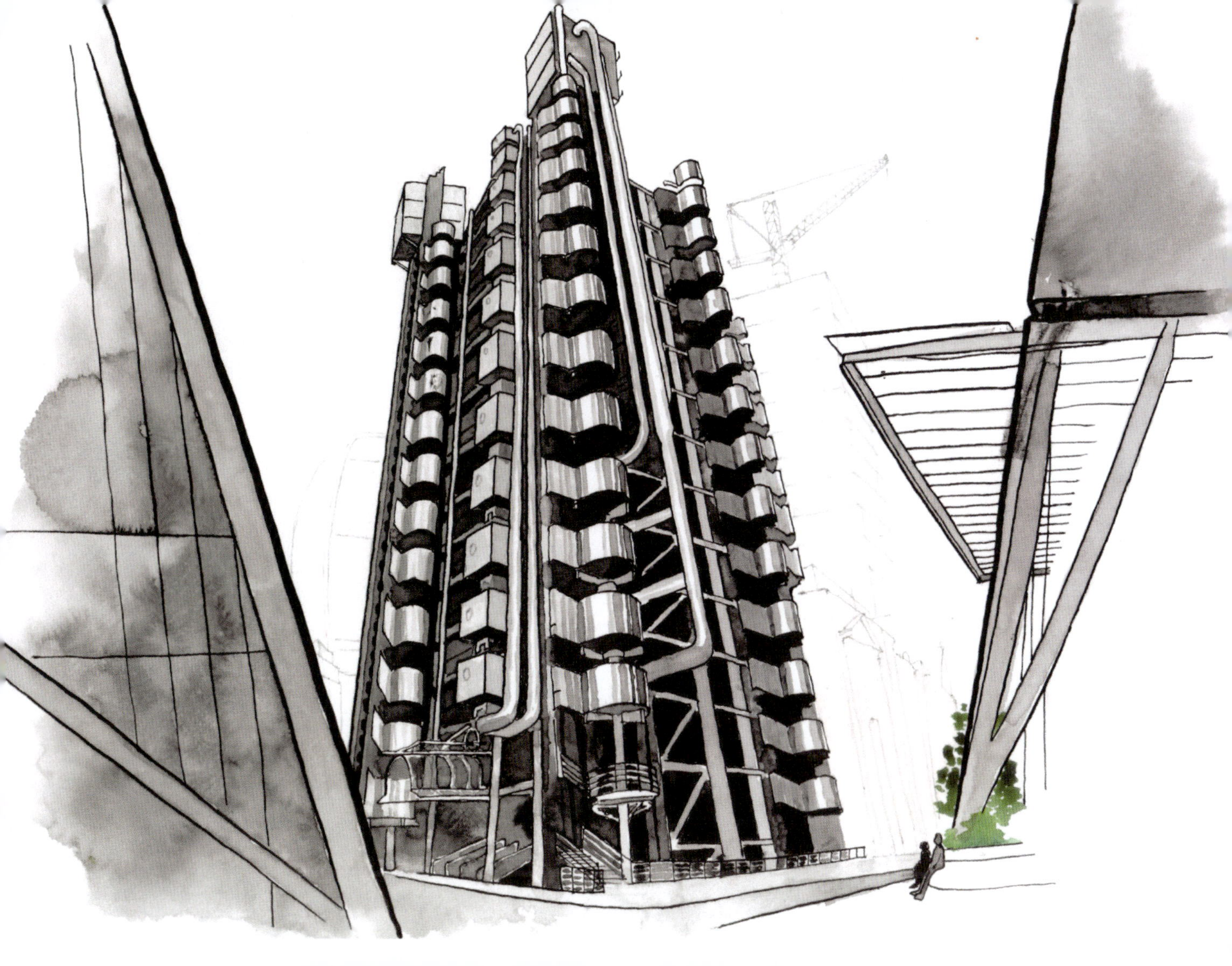

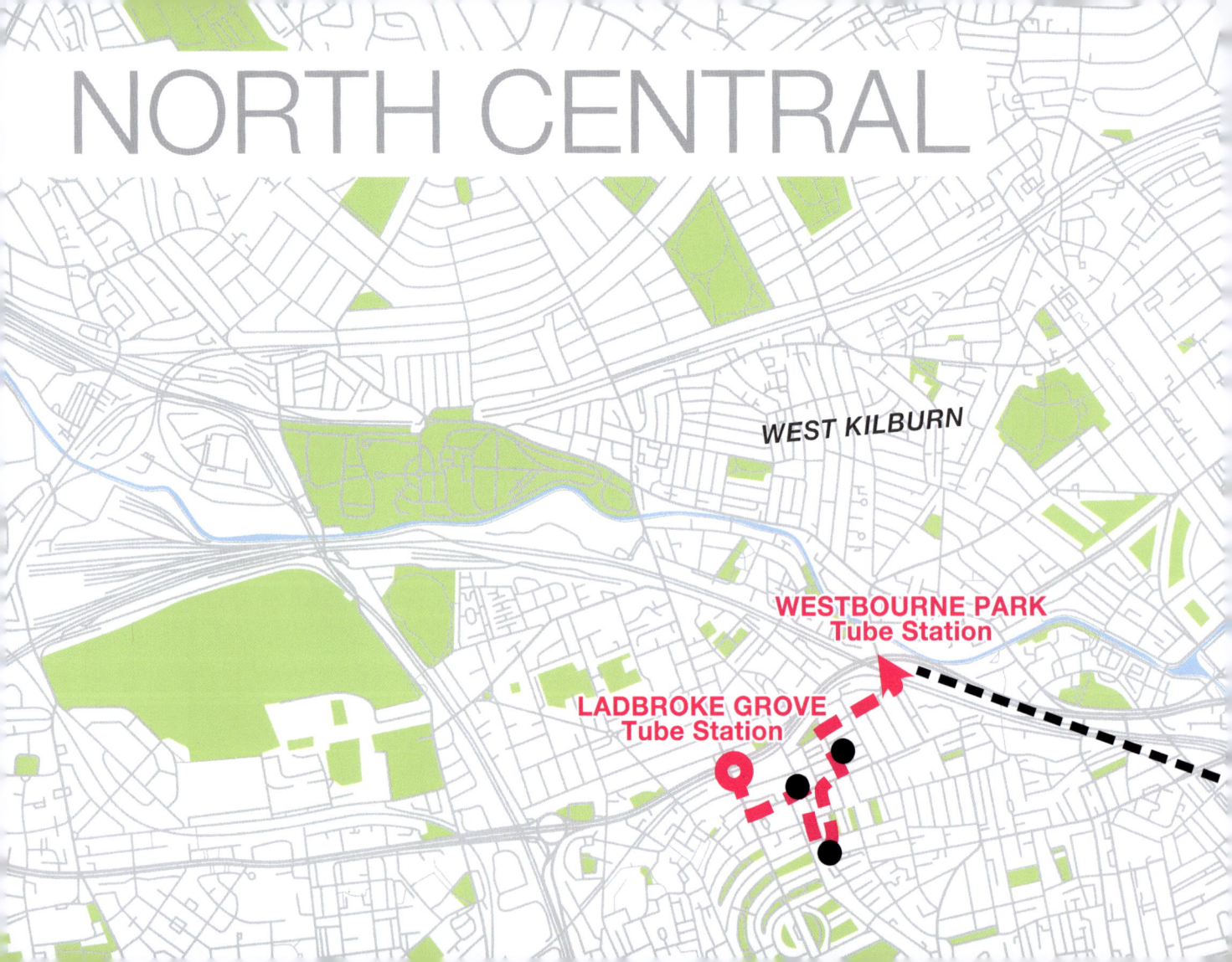

NORTH CENTRAL

WEST KILBURN

WESTBOURNE PARK Tube Station

LADBROKE GROVE Tube Station

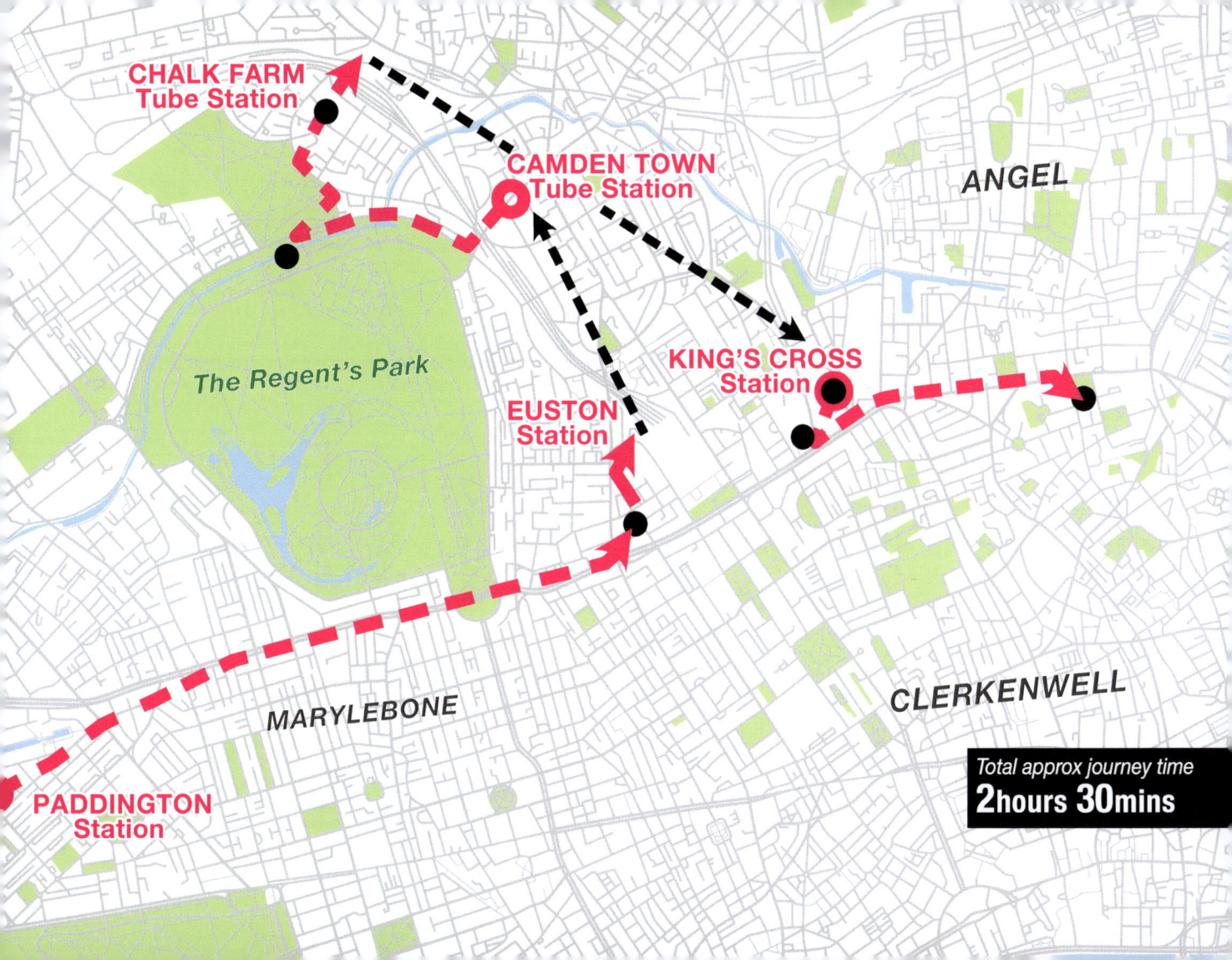

CHALK FARM Tube Station

CAMDEN TOWN Tube Station

ANGEL

The Regent's Park

KING'S CROSS Station

EUSTON Station

MARYLEBONE

CLERKENWELL

PADDINGTON Station

Total approx journey time
2hours 30mins

▶▶ THE WALKING GUIDE TO LONDON FILM SITES

NORTH CENTRAL

The enchanting worlds of a talking bear and a schoolboy wizard are among the fascinating film locations you'll encounter when you travel from west London to the north of the capital

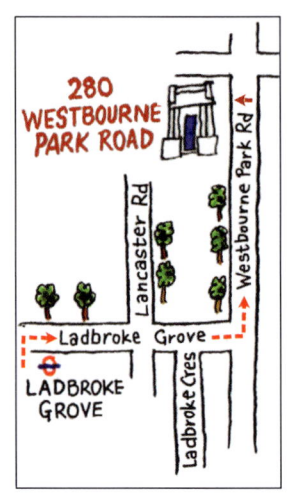

NOTTING HILL (1999)
280 Westbourne Park Road W11 1EH

Getting there
Start your journey by taking the train to Ladbroke Grove Tube Station. Turn right out of the station onto **Ladbroke Grove**. Continue along the road, across **Lancaster Road**, and pass **Ladbroke Crescent** on your right. Turn left onto **Westbourne Park Road**. Number 280 is just before the junction with **Portobello Road**. *(journey time 5 mins)*

The plot
Number 280 is the home of bookseller William Thacker (Hugh Grant) who falls in love with Hollywood star Anna Scott (Julia Roberts) in the romcom. Will bumps into Anna while turning the corner of the street and spills juice over her. The clumsy divorcee takes her to his flat to clean up and, as she leaves, she spontaneously kisses him. The building was chosen as a location because it was owned by the film's writer Richard Curtis.

Other starring roles
Just down the road at 223 Westbourne Park Road was the location where Teddy (Freddie Starr) enjoys chicken and chip as he meets his friend Jim Naboth (Stacy Keach) in the crime drama *The Squeeze* (1977).

A large part of *The L-Shaped Room* (1962), the award-winning Bryan Forbes romantic drama starring Leslie Caron and Tom Bell, was filmed in and around Westbourne Park Road. The boarding house in "Brockash Road", where Caron's character, a young French woman who is unmarried and pregnant, moves to, is St Luke's Road, off Westbourne Park Road.

Background
Notting Hill, after decades of gentrification is now one of the most fashionable areas of London but until the late 1970s much of it was a dilapidated district filled with cheap lodging houses. Charles Booth, the 19th century social reformer, went as far as to describe Golborne, just 10 minutes' walk to the north of Westbourne Park Road, as "one of the worst areas of London. Ten

minutes' walk to the east of the road was the home where serial killer John Christie carried out his murders. The building, made famous in the Richard Attenborough film **10 Rillington Place** (1971), no longer exists, however, having been demolished in 1970. The redevelopment of the area in the 1960s and 1970s saw the slums pulled down and the character of the district completely change as upper middle-class Londoners moved in and a large number of independent shops, restaurants and cafes opened.

▸▸ *Continue your film journey to* **PORTOBELLO ROAD**

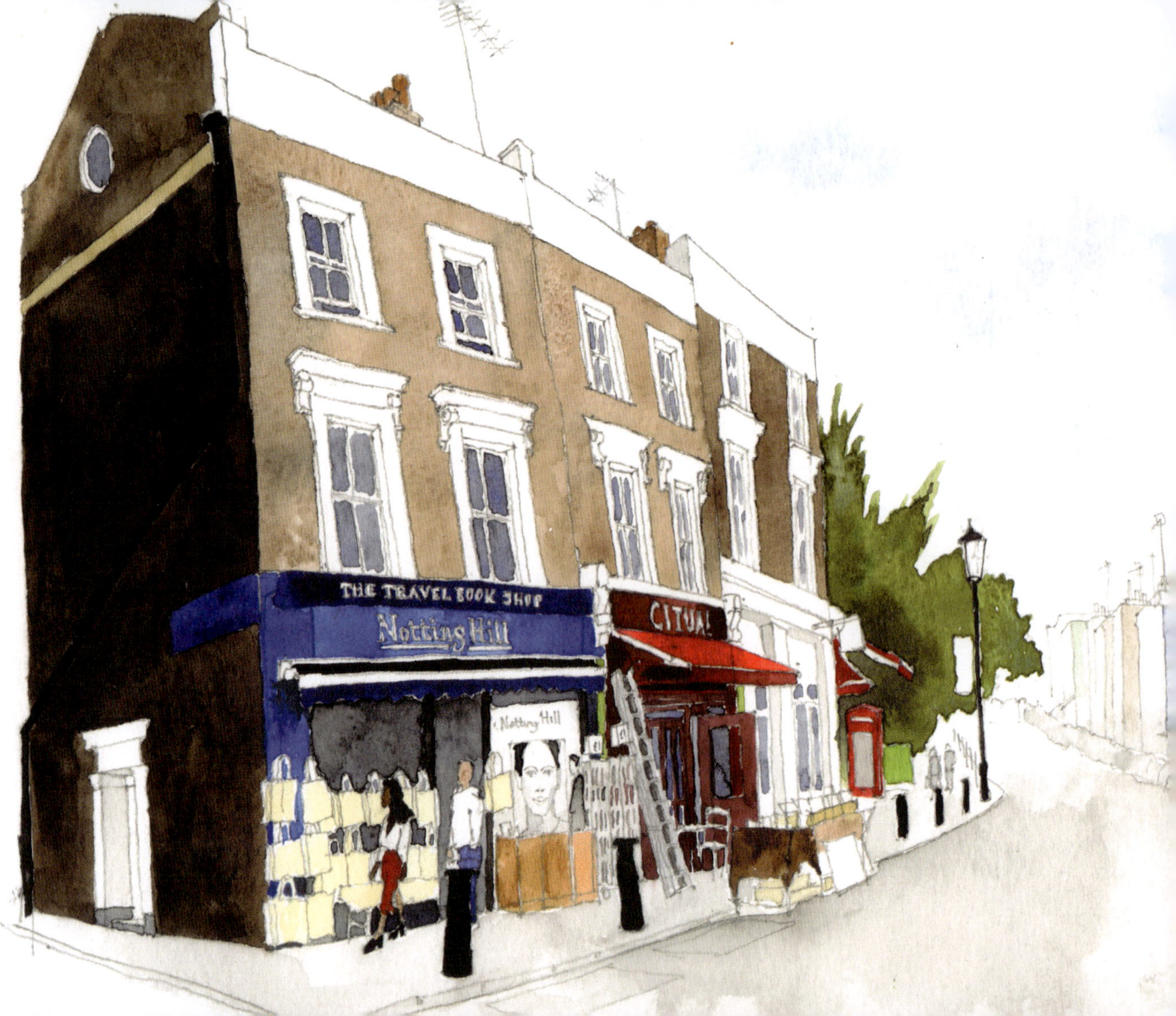
THE TRAVEL BOOK SHOP
Notting Hill

▶▶ THE WALKING GUIDE TO LONDON FILM SITES

NOTTING HILL (1999)
142 Portobello Road, London W11 2D2

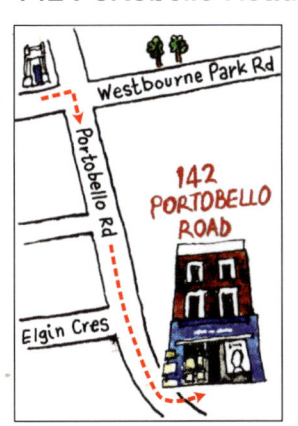

Getting there
From number 280, turn right at the end of **Westbourne Park Road** into **Portobello Road.** Pass **Blenheim Crescent** and **Elgin Crescent** on your right and you'll find number 142 on the left. *(journey time 4 min)*

The plot
142 Portobello Road was the location used for the Travel Bookshop where William Thacker (Hugh Grant) and Anna Scott (Julia Roberts) first met in the film but there was never a book shop there. Today it's a gift shop, but for fans of the film there's a sign on the front of the building saying, "The Travel book shop". Richard Curtis was inspired to write the film after frequently visting a bookshop at 13 Blenheim Crescent, just off Portobello Road, near to his home. The owner wouldn't allow filming in the shop, so the interior was reconstructed at Pinewood Studios.

Other starring roles
In *Cruella* (2021) Estella takes a stroll down Portobello Road and sees a Baroness dress in the window of the "2nd Time Around" shop. Further down the road at number 86 Portobello Road, "Gruber's" antique shop in *Paddington* (2014) is actually Alice's Antiques, a long-established business in the famous street.

Background
Portobello Road was much like every other London market, largely selling food and other essentials, until the 1940s when a growing number of rag-and-bone men started trading in the area. Increasingly the market became known for selling antiques. In the 1960s Portobello Road became famous as a place for trendsetters, like the Beatles and the Rolling Stones, to be seen. The main market day is Saturday, the only day when the whole market is open.

▶▶ *Continue your film journey to* **ST LUKES MEWS**

▶▶ THE WALKING GUIDE TO LONDON FILM SITES

LOVE ACTUALLY (2003)
27 St Lukes Mews W11 1DF

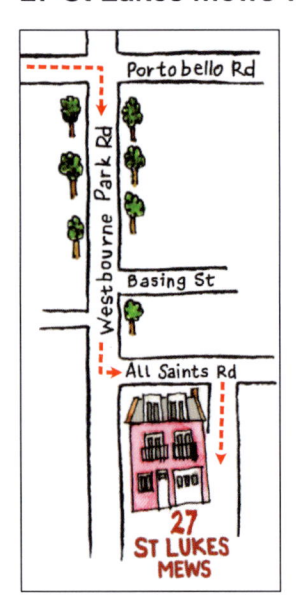

Getting there
From **Portobello Road**, back track to **Westbourne Park Road**, turn right and walk away from **Portobello Road** in the opposite direction from number 280, passing **Basing Street** on your left and **Clydesdale Road** on your right. Take the next left into **All Saints Road. St Lukes Mews** is first on your right.
(journey time 5 mins)

The plot
The famous scene from the Richard Curtis romcom where Mark (Andrew Lincoln) turns up on Christmas Eve armed with a boombox and a set of cards was shot at St Lukes Mews. While her husband Peter (Chiwetel Ejiofor) watches TV, outside in the mews, cue card by cue card, Mark spells out his love for Juliet (Keira Knightley). As he walks off, she races after him and kisses him tenderly on the lips. In the scene, inspired by Bob Dylan's video for *Subterranean Homesick Blues*, Andrew Lincoln actually handwrote the cards himself.

Other starring roles
London's mews houses have been regular locations for many years and were particularly popular in 1960s and 1970s TV series, exemplifying fashionable London in series such as **The Avengers** (1961), **The Saint** (1962) and **The Persuaders** (1971).

Ennismore Gardens Mews, near the Royal Albert Hall, was a particular favourite, appearing in series such as **The Sweeney** (1975) and **The Professionals** (1977) and Hitchcock's penultimate film **Frenzy** (1972), where it serves as the exterior of murder victim Brenda Blaney's (Barbara Leigh-Hunt) flat. It also featured in the Toni Collette comedy **Foster** (2011).

Queen's Gate Mews in nearby Kensington was the home of Daniel Craig's drug dealer character in **Layer Cake** (2004), while Stanhope Mews South in South Kensington boasts the house belonging to spymaster Harry (Colin Firth) in **Kingsman: The Secret Service** (2014).

Background
Mews houses were originally built as courtyards of stables and carriage houses to cater for the horses, coach men and stable staff of wealthy Londoners during the Georgian and Victorian ages. The ground floor normally consisted of a stable and a coach house, with a hay loft on the first floor along with accommodation for coach drivers and grooms. The word

▶▶ *Continue your film journey to* **PADDINGTON STATION** *or take a detour to* **SHEPHERD'S BUSH**

"mews" is first recorded as having been used to refer to stables as far back as 1548 and derived from the Royal Mews, a set of royal stables that were built 500 years ago on the site of a former hawk mews, a birdhouse for birds of prey.

SUGGESTED DETOUR →

The Gentlemen (2019)
The Princess Victoria, 217 Uxbridge Road, Shepherd's Bush, London W12 9DH

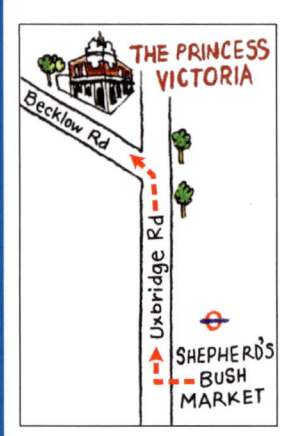

Getting there
While travelling through Westbourne Park Underground Station, you can make a detour to visit the Princess Victoria pub. Take the Circle/ Metropolitan Line south to Shepherd's Bush Market. Exit onto **Uxbridge Road** and continue along the road for almost 15 minutes, until you reach **Becklow Road** on the left. The Princess Victoria is on the corner of the two streets. *(journey time 25 mins, one way)*

The plot
When word gets around that American drugs baron Mickey Pearson (Matthew McConaughey), who has made a fortune cultivating and selling marijuana, is interested in selling his business all hell breaks loose in the London underworld. Pearson runs his business from the Princess Victoria, where he meets business partners and where much of the film's action takes place.

Other starring roles
Shepherd's Bush was the location for many iconic scenes in the cult music film **Quadrophenia** (1979). Jimmy (Phil Daniels) gives Steph (Leslie Ash) a ride on his Lambretta along Goldhawk Road, a short walk from Uxbridge Road, while rocker Kevin (Ray Winstone) is chased through a lane in Shepherd's Bush Market and eventually beaten up by a group of Mods.

The Dimco Buildings, that now sits between the White City Bus Station and the giant Westfield Shopping Centre, may still be identifiable to fans of **Who Framed Roger Rabbit** (1988) as the Acme Factory where the film's climactic scenes take place.

Background
For more than 100 years Shepherd's Bush has been an important popular culture centre in London. The Shepherd's Bush Empire, opened in 1903, featured many of the top theatre performers of the day, including a young Charlie Chaplin. It was later bought by the BBC, renamed BBC Television Theatre, and used to record audience-based TV series, including light entertainment shows featuring top stars of the day such as Cilla Black, Cliff Richard and Shirley Bassey. Until 2013 BBC Television also had its HQ in White City, to the north side of Shepherd's Bush, and just a short distance from there is White City Place, where many TV programmes are now produced by the BBC and independent production companies.

THE PRINCESS VICTORIA

▶▶ THE WALKING GUIDE TO LONDON FILM SITES

PADDINGTON (2014)
Paddington Station, Praed Street, London W2 1HU

Getting there
Exit **St Lukes Mews** and turn right up **All Saints Road**. Crossing **Lancaster Road** and passing **McGregor Road** on your right, turn into the next right, **Tavistock Road**. At the end of **Tavistock Road**, turn left into **Great Western Road**. At Westbourne Park Underground Station ahead of you, take a Circle/Hammersmith train to Paddington. Follow the signs for the mainline station. *(journey time 20 mins)*

The plot
Encouraged by his Aunt Lucy (voiced by Imelda Staunton) to leave the Peruvian jungle to start a new life in England, Paddington Bear (voiced by Ben Whishaw) makes the long journey to London and arrives at Paddington Station, where he is found by Mr and Mrs Brown (Hugh Bonneville and Sally Hawkins). Unable to ignore the label around his neck reading "Please look after this bear. Thank you." they adopt him and take him to live with them and their children. The actual station is used as a location for the film, but only for interior shots as the grander exterior of Marylebone Station was used for exterior filming. A sculpture of Paddington by artist Marcus Cornish now stands on Platform 1 under the station clock, near where the Browns first found the young bear.

Other starring roles
Daniel Craig's drug-dealer character greets northern hitman Mr Lucky (Paul Orchard) from the train at Paddington Station as part of his plan to kill Serbian assassin Dragan (Dragan Micanovic) in the crime drama **Layer Cake** (2004).
In the heist thriller **The Bank Job** (2008), based on the 1971 burglary of Lloyds Bank safety deposit boxes in Baker Street, Jason Statham's character, car salesman Terry Leather, meets up with gangster Lew Vogel (David Suchet) at the station to exchange incriminating documents.

Background
Paddington Station is the London terminus for trains to the South-west of England and Wales. The current station, built by Victorian engineering genius Isambard Kingdom Brunel, dates back to 1854, when it replaced a previous station built 16 years earlier. Much of Brunel's original design remains today and a statue of the engineer was erected on the concourse in his honour in 1982. The line into the station was the scene of a major disaster in 1999 which killed 31 people.

▶▶ *Continue your film journey to* **NORTH GOWER STREET**

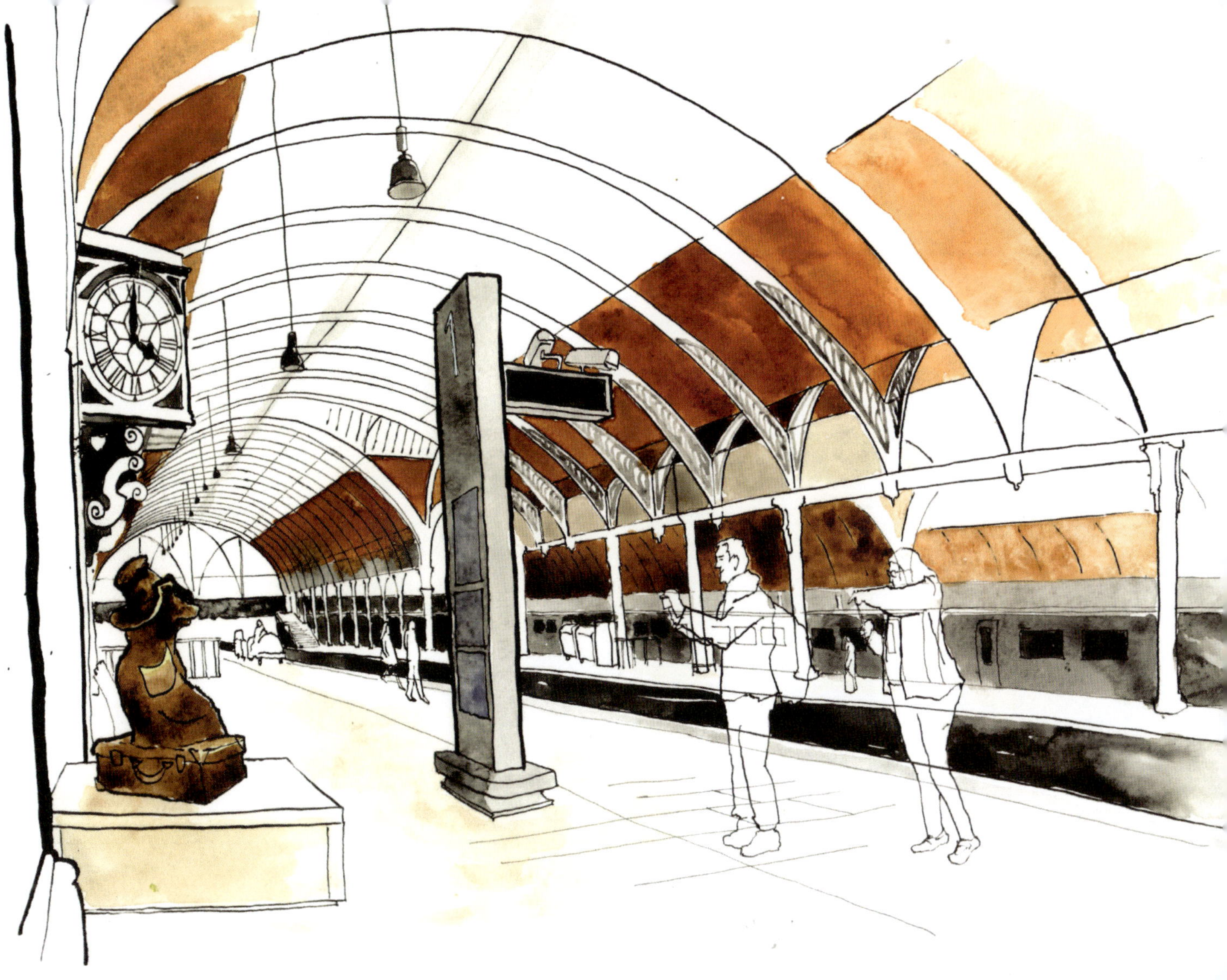

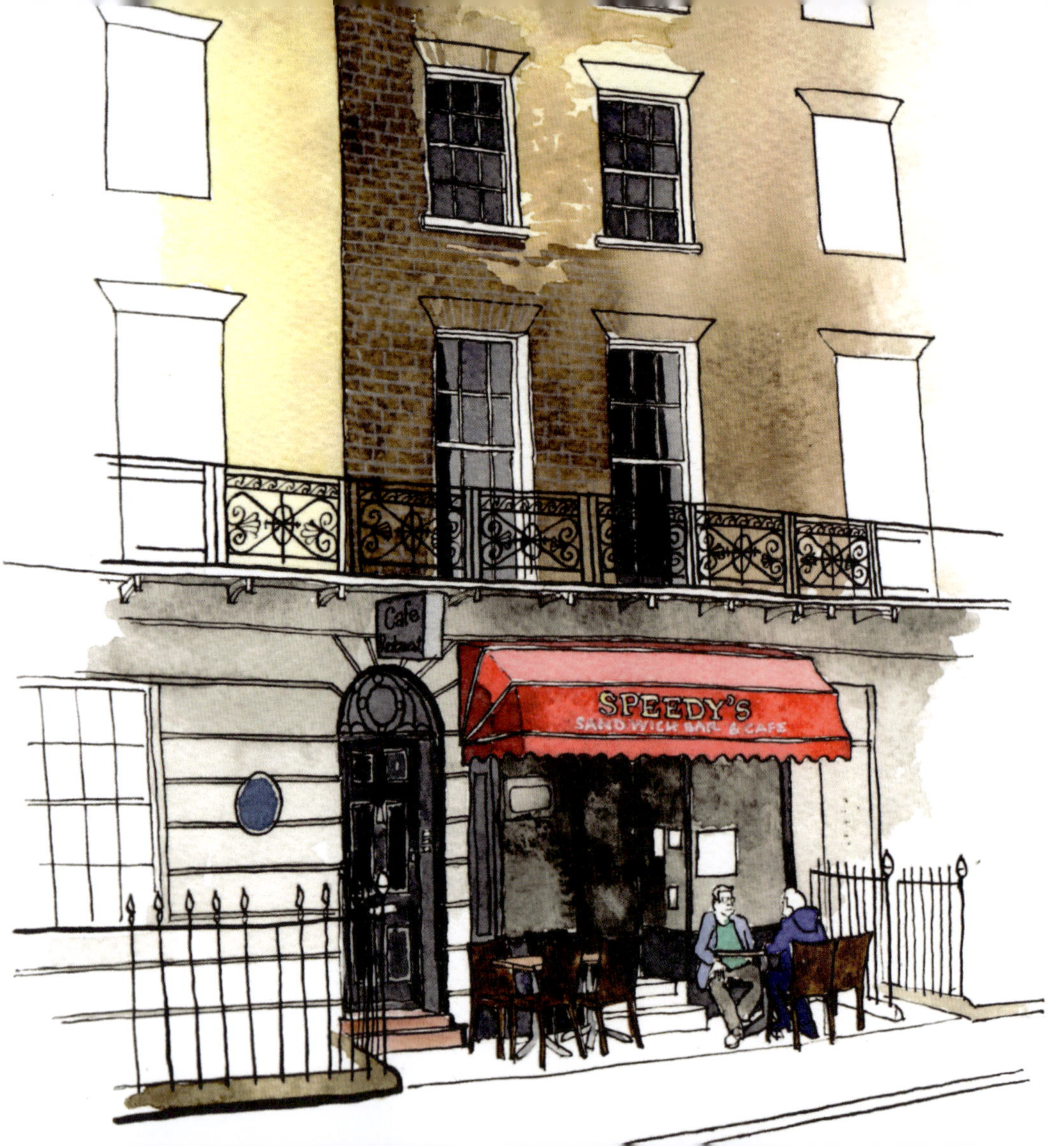
Cafe
SPEEDY'S
SANDWICH BAR & CAFE

SHERLOCK (2010)
187 North Gower Street, London NW1 2NJ

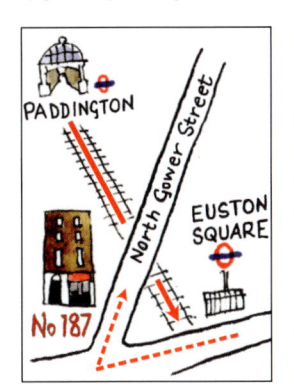

Getting there
Take a Circle or Hammersmith Tube from Paddington Station to Euston Square Station. Exiting the **North Gower Street** entrance, turn right and immediately right again into **North Gower Street**. Number 187 is on your left, just after **Tolmer's Square**.
(journey time 18 mins)

The plot
The house in North Gower Street plays the part of Sherlock Holmes' famous 221B Baker Street home in the TV series starring Benedict Cumberbatch as Holmes and Martin Freeman as Doctor Watson. The pair share the property with their housekeeper Mrs Hudson (Una Stubbs). Only the exterior of the building appears in the series, the inside of Sherlock's flat was filmed in a studio in Cardiff. The success of the series has also had a knock-on effect for Speedy's Cafe which is on the ground floor of number 187, with fans from around the world popping in for a refreshment. The blue plaque commemorating former resident Italian politician and activist Giuseppe Mazzini was covered by a fake lamp during filming.

Other starring roles
Many films have been shot in and around University College in Gower Street, just across the Euston Road from North Gower Street. It's a favourite location due to the historical character of University College's main building. In **The Mummy Returns** (2001) the Front Quad stands in for the British Museum. Christopher Nolan's **Inception** (2010) also uses the Front Quad as a location, along with the impressive interior of the college.

The college's Senate House makes an appearance in **Batman Begins** (2005) as the Gotham courthouse where Joe Chill (Richard Brake), killer of Bruce Wayne's parents, is gunned down as Bruce (Gus Lewis) watches.

Background
North Gower Street is the northern continuation of Gower Street, across the other side of Euston Road from the main street. Gower Street is named after Lady Gertrude Leveson-Gower, who in 1737 became the second wife of Lord John Russell, who owned the area. Over the years Gower Street has been home to a number of famous residents, including Charles Darwin and Charles Dickens, whose mother opened a school in the street when the writer was a child.

▶▶ *Continue your film journey towards* **LONDON ZOO REPTILE HOUSE**

▶▶ THE WALKING GUIDE TO LONDON FILM SITES

HARRY POTTER AND THE PHILOSOPHER'S (SORCERER'S) STONE (2001)
London Zoo Reptile House, Outer Circle, London NW1 4RY

Getting there
Continue up **North Gower Street** a few yards and turn right into **Euston Street**. Head along the street until you reach Euston Station. Take the Northern Line Tube to Camden Town Station. Exit left onto **Camden High Street**. Turn immediately right onto **Parkway** and pass **Arlington Road** and **Albert Street** on your left. Cross two junctions and then continue to the right along **Gloucester Gate** as the road forks, just across the bridge. Turn right onto **Outer Circle**. Continue for some way until the zoo entrance appears on your left.
(journey time 32 mins)

The plot
The Dursleys visit London Zoo with their son Dudley (Harry Melling) and reluctantly take Harry along too. When Harry (Daniel Radcliffe) is left alone in the Reptile House, he realises that he can talk to snakes and has a conversation with a python through the glass of its enclosure. When Dudley pushes Harry out of the way, the young wizard makes the glass vanish and Dudley falls through into the enclosure. The snake escapes and as it leaves it thanks Harry.

Other starring roles
The scene in *An America Werewolf in London* (1981), where David (David Naughton) wakes up naked in the zoo was shot at London Zoo. While another 1980s British cult classic *Withnail and I* (1987) ends with Richard E Grant performing Hamlet for the unimpressed wolves in the Wolves House at the zoo.

Visiting the zoo in *About a Boy* (2002), Will (Hugh Grant) attempts to convince 12-year-old Marcus (Nicholas Hoult) to pretend to be his son so he can hook up with a woman he wants to get to know.

Background
London Zoo is the world's oldest scientific zoo, opened in 1828. It has been home to many notable residents. These included Obaysch, the first hippopotamus to be seen in Europe since the Roman Empire when he arrived in the mid 19th century, and the only living quagga, a kind of zebra, ever to be photographed, before the species became extinct in 1883. Another resident, Jumbo the elephant, became a huge celebrity in the 1860s, even spawning the word "jumbo" meaning large, as in jumbo jet or jumbo packet.

▶▶ *Continue your film journey to* **CHALCOT CRESCENT** *or take a detour to* **HIGHGATE CEMETERY**

SUGGESTED DETOUR →

Fantastic Beasts: The Crimes of Grindelwald (2018)
Highgate Cemetery, Swain's Lane N6 6PJ

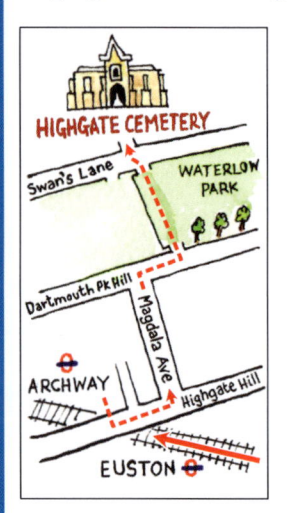

Getting there
While travelling through Euston Station, you can make a detour to Highgate Cemetery. Take the Northern Line from Euston to Archway Tube Station. Exit via the **Highgate Hill** entrance, climb the stairs and turn left. Head up the road, crossing **MacDonald Road**, and turn down **Magdala Avenue** on the left, just before Whittington Hospital. Continue along the road until the crossroads at the end. Turn right into **Dartmouth Park Road** and continue until you reach Waterlow Park gates on your left. Keeping to your left, follow the path through the park. The cemetery is opposite the exit gate. *(journey time 25 mins, one way)*

The plot
In the sequel to *Fantastic Beasts and Where to Find Them* (2016), Albus Dumbledore (Jude Law) recruits his former student Newt Scamander (Eddie Redmayne) as he attempts to stop Grindelwald's (Johnny Depp) plans of raising pure-blood wizards to rule over all non-magical beings. Grindelwald summons his followers to a rally at the Lestrange family mausoleum in the famous Cimetière du Père-Lachaise in Paris. The scenes were filmed around the tombs in the Circle of Lebanon in North London's Highgate Cemetery.

Other starring roles
The Circle of Lebanon was also featured in *Dorian Gray* (2009), the film adaptation of Oscar Wilde's novel, starring Ben Barnes and Colin Firth.

Highgate has been a favourite location for many horror films, including Peter Cushing's *Frankenstein and the Monster from Hell* (1974), *Taste the Blood of Dracula* (1970), with Christopher Lee, and *The Abominable Dr Phibes* (1971), starring Vincent Price.

Julien Temple's mockumentary *The Great Rock 'n' Roll Swindle* (1980), starring the Sex Pistols and their manager Malcolm McLaren, also featured a sequence filmed in the Circle of Lebanon.

Background
Highgate Cemetery, opened in 1839, is the resting place of a huge number of famous figures, including philosopher and politician Karl Marx. The Circle of Lebanon is a series of 20 tombs built around the roots of an ancient Cedar of Lebanon tree, which gives the circle its name. Tours of the cemetery are available to book.

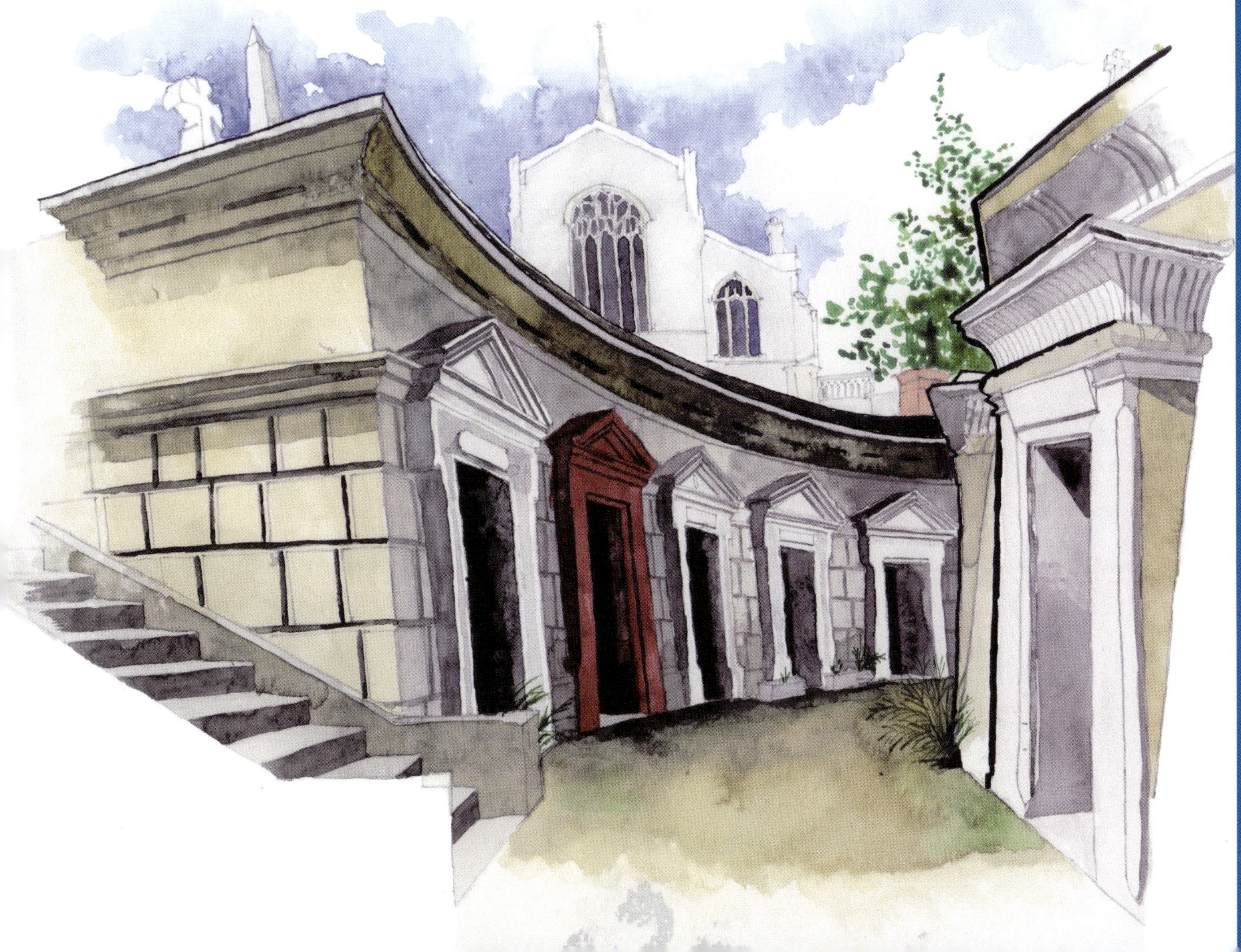

▶▶ THE WALKING GUIDE TO LONDON FILM SITES

PADDINGTON (2014)
30 Chalcot Crescent, London NW1 8YD

Getting there
Outside London Zoo's main entrance, turn right and backtrack along **Outer Circle** on the left-hand side of the street until you see a path just after the Royal Zoological Society of London building. Follow the path across a small bridge until you reach **Prince Albert Road**. Cross the road and continue up **St Mark's Square**, with St Mark's church on your right. At the crossroads, turn left onto **Regent's Park Road** (confusingly initially also signposted **St Mark's Square**) and continue past **Fitzroy Road** on the right until you reach **Chalcot Crescent**. Number 30 is on the right as the road begins to bend. *(journey time 14 mins)*

The plot
After finding Paddington (voiced by Ben Whishaw) at the station, the Brown family take the bear back to their large terraced home at 32 Windsor Gardens, just around the corner from the station. There is actually a real Windsor Gardens in London, but it has no connection to the books or films and Chalcot Crescent was the location used to film the Brown's home. Mr Brown (Hugh Bonneville) doesn't believe Paddington's story about how he found himself in London and insists the bear only stays with them for one night. His wife, the children and their housekeeper, Mrs Bird (Julie Walters), however, are enchanted by the young bear. When the Brown family leave Paddington alone in the house, evil museum taxidermist Millicent Clyde (Nicole Kidman), who kills and stuffs animals for the museum, sneaks in and attempts to capture the little bear.

Other starring roles
Primrose Hill, the public park just west of Chalcot Crescent, is a favourite location for films, largely due to its wonderful views of London. The opening scene of **Bridget Jones: The Edge of Reason** (2004) shows Bridget dancing with Mark Darcy on Primrose Hill itself, in a parody of **The Sound of Music** (1965).

In the film version of Frederick Forsyth's spy novel **The Fourth Protocol** (1987), the hill, with its distinctive backdrop of London, is used for a clandestine meeting between British secret service chief Sir Nigel Irvine (Ian Richardson) and MI5's John Preston (Michael Caine).

Background
Primrose Hill, a Grade II listed park which includes one of six protected viewpoints in London,

first opened to the public in 1842. Prior to that date it was best known as the venue for personal duels between gentlemen. Due to its growing popularity in the 19th century, the whole district, including Chalcot Crescent, was also named Primrose Hill.

The area has had many famous residents, including the poet and novelist Sylvia Plath and her husband poet Ted Hughes, who lived in a flat at 3 Chalcot Square, just a short walk from Paddington's "home". The building is marked with a blue plaque to commemorate their residency. Plaques also mark the former homes of other historic local personalities, including philosopher Friedrich Engels, broadcaster AJP Taylor and photographer Roger Fenton.

▶▶ *Continue your film journey towards* **KING'S CROSS STATION**

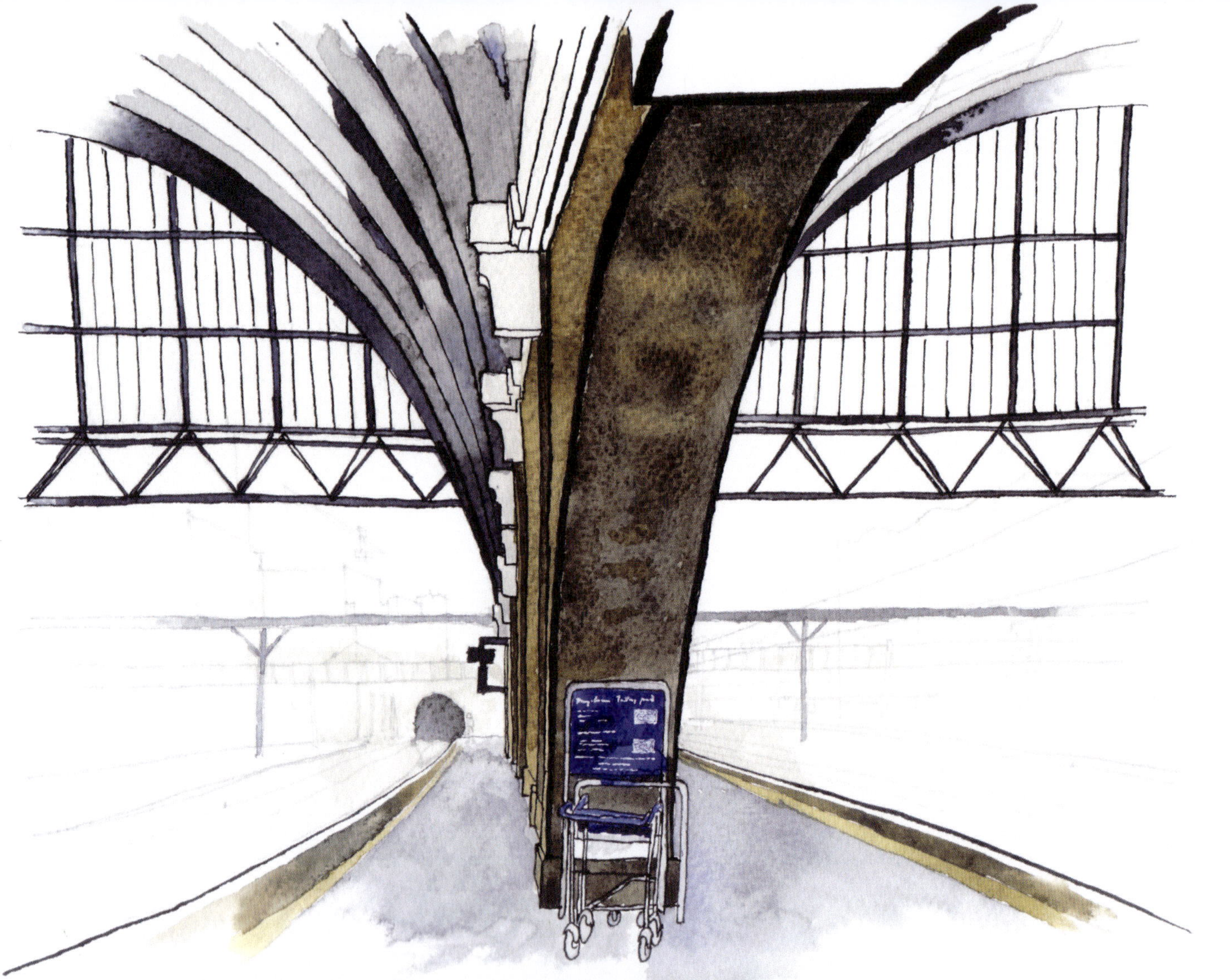

▶▶ THE WALKING GUIDE TO LONDON FILM SITES

HARRY POTTER AND THE PHILOSOPHER'S (SORCERER'S) STONE (2001)
King's Cross Station, London N1 9AL

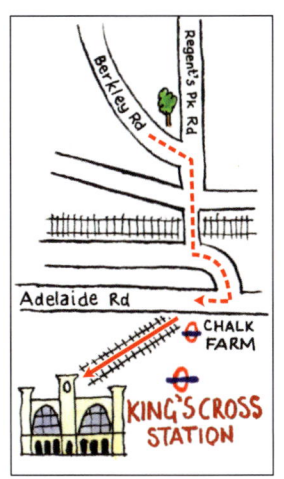

Getting there
Continue along the right-hand side of **Chalcot Crescent**, past **Chalcot Square** on your right, until it becomes **Berkley Road** and meets **Regent's Park Road**. Turn right onto **Regent's Park Road** and cross the bridge at the top of the road. Continue straight ahead as the road becomes **Bridge Approach** and turn right at the junction at the top into **Adelaide Road**. A short distance on the left enter Chalk Farm Underground Station and take a Northern Line train to King's Cross Station. Follow the signs to the mainline station. *(journey time 28 mins)*

The plot
At the beginning of the first Harry Potter film, Harry (Daniel Radcliffe) is heading for Hogwarts School of Witchcraft and Wizardry and, with the school's other students, reaches the train by running through a brick wall between Platforms 9 and 10, a secret entrance to Platform 9¾, where the Hogwarts Express is located. Author JK Rowling has revealed there's a romantic reason why she chose King's Cross as the starting point for Harry's journey, as it's where her parents first met on a train to Scotland. If you visit the station, look out for a sign reading "Platform 9¾" where a luggage trolley is embedded in the wall. It's free to take photographs.

Other starring roles
In **Mission: Impossible – Rogue Nation** (2015), the fifth MI film, Benji (Simon Pegg) is kidnapped in King's Cross Station, although the production team's set dressing means the actual station looks very different from how it is seen on camera.

King's Cross stood in for another London station, Paddington, in **Wonder Woman** (2017). Paddington's extensive modernisation meant it couldn't play itself in the scenes where Diana (Gal Gadot) tastes her first ice cream and the troops head for France in 1918.

Background
The area where King's Cross Station sits has a history going back to Roman times and legend has it that the Celtic warrior queen Boudica fought her last battle on the site. The station was opened in 1852 and is the London terminus serving the East Coast Main Line to Yorkshire and the Humber, North-east England and Scotland. The station was the site of a deadly blaze in 1987 when a fire under a wooden escalator quickly spread, killing 31 people.

▶▶ *Continue your film journey to* **ST PANCRAS STATION**

96

▶▶ THE WALKING GUIDE TO LONDON FILM SITES

HARRY POTTER AND THE CHAMBER OF SECRETS (2002)
St Pancras Renaissance Hotel, London NW1 2AR

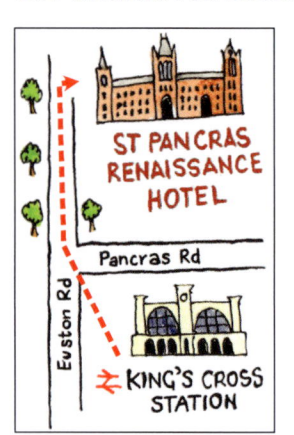

Getting there
Leave the main entrance of **King's Cross Station** onto **Euston Road**. Turn right and cross **Pancras Road**. Continue along the road until the entrance to the hotel appears on your right.
(journey time 4 min)

The plot
In the second Harry Potter film, when Harry (Daniel Radcliffe) and Ron Weasley (Rupert Grint) can't enter Platform 9¾, Ron decides to fly his father's blue Ford Anglia car to catch up with the train. The car is parked outside the hotel, which in the film plays the role of the entrance to King's Cross Station but in reality is part of the adjacent Victorian St Pancras Station complex. As the car lifts into the air and flies away, St Pancras can be seen in the background below.

Other starring roles
Peter Parker (Tom Holland) and his schoolmates arrive in the UK at St Pancras International station, as it's now known, in **Spider-Man: Far From Home** (2019).

Cruella de Vil travels in the opposite direction from St Pancras, heading to Paris on the Orient Express, in the live-action sequel **102 Dalmatians** (2000).

Romcoms **Bridget Jones's Baby** (2016) and **I Give It a Year** (2013) feature St Pancras. In the first, Bridget (Renée Zellweger) meets a friend there to head off to a festival, while in the latter Josh (Rafe Spall) professes his love for Chloe (Anne Faris) as she's about to leave on a romantic trip to Paris with Guy (Simon Baker).

Background
St Pancras Station opened in 1868 but changed its title to St Pancras International in 2007, when trains to mainland Europe began running from the station.

The name St Pancras comes from the surrounding St Pancras church district which derives from the fourth-century child martyr Pancras of Rome.

The Midland Grand Hotel was opened by the Midland Railway Company next to its railway station in 1873 and after it closed in 1935 was mainly used as offices until part of the original building was reopened as the St Pancras Renaissance London Hotel in 2011.

The station itself hosts a number of works of public art, including the nine-metre tall The Meeting Place, underneath the station clock, which shows a couple embracing, and is said to have been designed to convey the romance of travel.

▶▶ *Continue your film journey to* **CLAREMONT SQUARE**

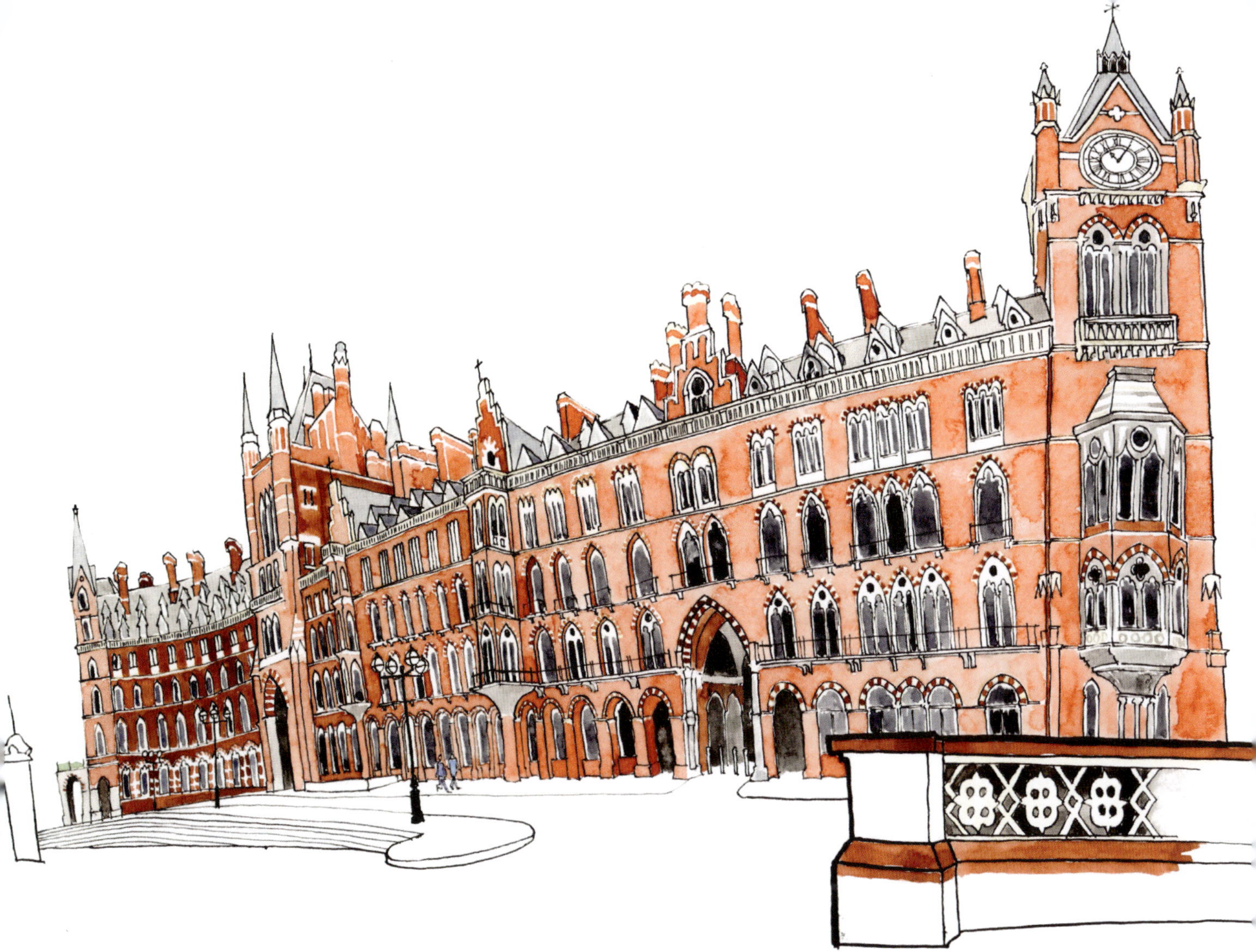

▶▶ THE WALKING GUIDE TO LONDON FILM SITES

HARRY POTTER AND THE ORDER OF THE PHOENIX (2007)

Claremont Square, London N1 9LX

Getting there
Backtrack along Euston Road, passing King's Cross Station on your left. Cross the traffic lights at the junction onto Pentonville Road. Continue along the road, passing nine streets on your left, including Caledonian Road and Rodney Street, until you reach Claremont Square on your right, turn into the square, then turn first left. *(journey time 18 mins)*

The plot
Claremont Square is the location where the exterior shots of 12 Grimmauld Place were shot. In the film, Grimmauld Place is the ancestral home of the Black family in London's Islington district and was invisible to Muggles (those who have no magical abilities). As they can't see number 12, local residents assume that the houses have been misnumbered and that nothing exists been number 11 and number 13. The house was also placed under a Fidelius Charm which meant that it could only be accessed by wizards to whom the Secret Keeper, Albus Dumbledore (Michael Gambon) until his death, had revealed its location. The property was inherited by Harry's (Daniel Radcliffe) godfather Sirius Black (Gary Oldman) and became the headquarters of the Order of the Phoenix. Harry later inherited the building when Sirius was murdered.

Other starring roles
The Portland Row headquarters of AJ Lockwood & Co investigators agency in the Netflix series *Lockwood & Co* (2023) was filmed at 33 Claremont Square.

Just a few streets away is 18 Lloyd Square, where another character played by Gary Oldman, spy master George Smiley, has his home in *Tinker Tailor Soldier Spy* (2011).

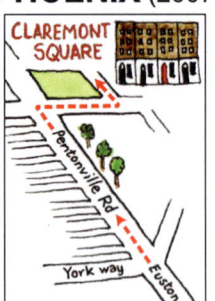

Less than a five-minute walk south of Claremont Square is Myddelton Square where Emmeline Pankhurst (Meryl Streep) delivers a rousing speech to her supporters in *Suffragette* (2015). The square has also been featured in other TV and film productions, including BBC's *Howards End* (2017) and *The End of the Affair* (1999).

Background
The Claremont Square houses used for filming were all built in the early 19th century. The square itself also holds another secret, beneath the mound in the centre is a hidden architectural treasure, an amazing example of an 18th century inner city reservoir that is still operational today.

99

Printed in Great Britain
by Amazon

51189189R00064